COMPACT MOSAIC I

A COMMUNICATION-BASED GRAMMAR

COMPACT MOSAIC I

A COMMUNICATION-BASED GRAMMAR

Patricia K. Werner
University of Wisconsin, Madison

With contributions by

Lida R. Baker
University of California, Los Angeles

Miki Prijic Knezevic

McGRAW-HILL, INC.

New York St. Louis San Francisco Auckland Bogotá Caracas
Lisbon London Madrid Mexico Milan Montreal New Delhi
Paris San Juan Singapore Sydney Tokyo Toronto

This is an EBI book.
Compact Mosaic I
A Communication-based Grammar

1 2 3 4 5 6 7 8 9 DOH DOH 9 0 9 8 7 6 5 4 3 2

ISBN: 0-07-069537-7

This book was set in 10/12 Aster by Progressive Typographers.
The designer was Jane Moorman.
The editors were Elaine Goldberg, Roseanne Mendoza, and Celine-Marie Pascale.
The production supervisor was Tanya Nigh.
The photo researcher was Judy Mason.
New drawings were done by Jim M'Guinness.
R.R. Donnelley and Sons Company was printer and binder.

Cover: Robert Delaunay, *Landscape with Disk*, 1905. Oil on canvas, 21⅜ × 18″. Photographie Musée National d'Art Moderne. Centre Georges Pompidou, Paris.

Library of Congress Cataloging-in-Publication Data

Werner, Patricia K., 1951–
    Compact mosaic I: a communication-based grammar / Patricia K.
Werner, with contributions by Lida R. Baker, Miki Prijic Knezevic.
        p.   cm.
    Includes index.
    ISBN 0-07-069537-7
    1. English language — Textbooks for foreign speakers.   2. English
language — Grammar — 1950–   I. Baker, Lida R.   II. Knezevic, Miki
Prijic, 1941–   III. Title.   IV. Title: Compact mosaic 1.
V. Title: Compact mosaic one.
PE1128.W426   1993
428.2'4 — dc20   91-29136
                                                                                             CIP

Grateful acknowledgment is made for use of the following:

Photographs: *Page 1* © Patricia Werner; *10* © Arthur Grace/Stock, Boston; *13* © Patricia Werner; *14* © Patricia Werner; *15* © Patricia Werner; *44* © Bonnie Freer/Photo Researchers, Inc.; *22* © Judy Gelles/Stock, Boston; *68* © Robert Houser/Comstock; *76 (top left)* © AT&T Archives; *76 (top right)* © AP/Wide World Photos; *80 (left)* © The Bettmann Archive; *80 (right)* © Apple Computers; *83* © Ray Ellis/Photo Researchers, Inc.; *86* © AP/Wide World Photos; *89* © Merrin/Monkmeyer; *115* © Ken Robert Buck/ Stock, Boston; *131* © Patricia Werner; *151* © Patricia Werner; *162* © Wide World Photos; *165* George Daniell Photo Researchers; *166 (left & right) Autumn Leaves,* Georgia O'Keeffe, Art Resource; *168* © AP/Wide World Photos; *171* © PA/Wide World Photos; *175* © UPI/Bettmann; *176 (left & right)* © AP/Wide World Photos; *177* © AP/Wide World Photos; *179* © Ernst Haas/Magnum; *189 Relativity* by M.C. Escher, National Gallery of Art, Washington. Gift of Mrs. C.V.S. Roosevelt; *191 (top)* © Rick Smolan/Stock, Boston; *191 (bottom)* © Paul Conklin; *192* © Alan Carey/The Image Works; *194* © J. Moore/The

Credits continue on page 273.

To all mothers (and especially to my mother)

Contents

About This Book   xi

CHAPTER 1

The Family   1

VERB TENSES

PART ONE   Simple Present and Present Continuous Tenses   3
PART TWO   Simple Past and Past Continuous Tenses, *When* and *While*   13
PART THREE   Future Tenses, *Be Going to*   22
PART FOUR   Present Perfect Continuous and Present Perfect Tenses   27
PART FIVE   *Used to, Would, Was/Were Going to;* Past Perfect Tense   35
PART SIX   **Language Activities**   41

CHAPTER 2

Health   44

MODAL AUXILIARIES AND RELATED STRUCTURES

PART ONE   Modals of Ability and Expectation   46
PART TWO   Modals of Request, Permission, and Preference   50
PART THREE   Modals of Need and Advice   55
PART FOUR   Modals of Possibility and Probability   61
PART FIVE   **Language Activities**   66

CHAPTER 3

Technology   68

THE PASSIVE VOICE

PART ONE   Passive Voice—Simple Tenses   70
PART TWO   Passive Voice—Perfect Tenses   77
PART THREE   Passive Voice—Continuous Tenses   80
PART FOUR   Passive Voice—Modal Auxiliaries   83
PART FIVE   **Language Activities**   86

CHAPTER 4

Money Matters   89

NOUNS, PRONOUNS, AND NOUN MODIFIERS

PART ONE   Count Nouns and Noncount Nouns; Indefinite Articles   91
PART TWO   Indefinite Adjectives and Pronouns   98
PART THREE   The Definite Article with Count and Noncount Nouns   104
PART FOUR   Units of Measurement   109
PART FIVE   **Language Activities**   113

CHAPTER 5

Leisure Time   115

GERUNDS, INFINITIVES, AND OTHER VERB FORMS

PART ONE   Forms of Gerunds and Infinitives; Prepositions Followed by Gerunds; Adjectives, Adverbs, and Nouns Followed by Infinitives   117
PART TWO   Verbs Followed by Gerunds or Infinitives   126
PART THREE   More Verbs Followed by Gerunds or Infinitives   130
PART FOUR   Verbs Followed by Either Gerunds or Infinitives   135
PART FIVE   Causative Verbs and Related Structures; Verbs of Perception; Present and Past Participles Used as Adjectives   141
PART SIX   **Language Activities**   148

CHAPTER 6

Creativity   151

ADVERB CLAUSES

PART ONE   Sentence Types, Coordinating Conjunctions, and Clauses of Time and Condition — Present and Future Time   154
PART TWO   Comparisons   162
PART THREE   Clauses and Related Structures Showing Cause, Contrast, Purpose, and Result or Effect   169
PART FOUR   Clauses of Time — Past Time   179
PART FIVE   **Language Activities**   187

CHAPTER 7
Human Behavior   191

ADJECTIVE CLAUSES
PART ONE   Adjective Clauses with *That, When,* and *Where* — Replacement of Subjects, Objects, and Adverbials of Time or Place   194
PART TWO   Restrictive and Nonrestrictive Clauses; Clauses with *Who, Which,* and *Whose* — Replacement of Subjects and Possessives   199
PART THREE   Adjective Clauses with *Who(m)* and *Which* — Replacement of Objects   207
PART FOUR   **Language Activities**   212

CHAPTER 8
Living Together on a Small Planet   216

NOUN CLAUSES AND CONDITIONAL SENTENCES
PART ONE   Noun Clauses and Reported Speech   218
PART TWO   Noun Clauses and Embedded Questions — Clause-to-Phrase Reduction   226
PART THREE   *Hope, Wish,* and Conditional Sentences — Present and Future Time   231
PART FOUR   Perfect Modal Auxiliaries and Conditional Sentences — Past and Past-to-Present Time   237
PART FIVE   **Language Activities**   245

APPENDICES
APPENDIX 1   Parts of Speech and Sentences   250
APPENDIX 2   Spelling Rules   254
APPENDIX 3   Summary of Modal Auxiliaries and Related Structures   260
APPENDIX 4   *The* with Proper Nouns   262
APPENDIX 5   Summary of Gerunds and Infinitives   264

INDEX   269

About This Book

Compact Mosaic I: A Communication-based Grammar is a multifunctional text for intermediate to high-intermediate students of English as a Second Language or for high-intermediate to advanced students of English as a Foreign Language. The core of the text is review and study of essential English grammar. Structures are not covered in isolation, however; they are introduced, practiced, and applied within familiar contexts. The goal of the text is not only to practice grammatical structures but also to use them as a means to communicate ideas.

Organization and Teaching Suggestions

Compact Mosaic I: A Communication-based Grammar is organized by grammatical structure and by theme. Thematically, each chapter develops a different topic chosen according to the frequency of use of particular structures within that topic.

All chapters begin with a reading that introduces the topic and highlights the structures covered in the chapter. These introductory readings are followed by questions on vocabulary and ideas for discussion. The readings may be assigned as homework, read silently or aloud in class, or used as listening passages.

Each part of a chapter includes a progression of exercises that develop content information while practicing the target structures. Most serve as either oral or written exercises and lend themselves to varied classroom organization: pairs, small groups, large groups, or whole class. In addition, with many exercises there is a section called Your Turn, which gives a way of personalizing the ideas from the exercises.

Each chapter ends with a range of activities designed to apply the structures covered in the chapter. The activities are meant to be loosely controlled by the teacher, allowing students to experiment with the structures they have been practicing. The activities range from games and role-plays to essays and poetry writing. The activities are optional, of course, but we heartily encourage their use.

Differences Between *Compact Mosaic I: A Communication-based Grammar* and *Mosaic I: A Content-based Grammar*

The shorter text, *Compact Mosaic I: A Communication-based Grammar*, differs from its predecessor in several ways. Above all, *Compact Mosaic I* is oriented even more to discussion and conversation, encouraging students *to use* specific grammatical structures and a range of new vocabulary in real communication.

In terms of organization and content, the new text has eight chapters with a total of forty-one parts. It covers high-frequency structures while eliminating lower frequency ones such as the future perfect tense. Eight reading selections are included, as opposed to over sixty in the original. Throughout the new text, exercises have been simplified and/or shortened, and much of the content of Chapters 6, 7, and 8 has been changed.

Dozens of people contributed their ideas, time, energy, and faith during the development of this text. The author is very grateful to all colleagues, friends, and family who helped, especially Lida Baker, Laurie Blass, Miki Knezevic, and John Nelson. Above all, thanks to Mary Gill, Roseanne Mendoza, and Elaine Goldberg for their long hours of work, support, and encouragement.

COMPACT MOSAIC I

A COMMUNICATION-BASED GRAMMAR

The Family

Verb Tenses

This chapter covers present, past, and future verb tenses, and it also includes the expressions *used to*, *would*, and *was/were going to*. Parts of the chapter may be a review for you, and **you may not need to study everything**. Concentrate on the structures you **need** to practice.

Previewing the Passage

Have you lived with or become close to an American family? From your experience, is the "typical" American family similar to or different from what you had heard or read about in the past?

What Is Happening to the American Family?

The American family is changing. In fact, today there isn't one typical American family, but rather there are many types of families. In the past, however, there were more or less typical U.S. families.

5   During the first half of this century, the "average" family had a mother, a father, and two or more children. In addition, aunts, uncles, and grandparents would often live with their relatives in extended family groups. In rural families, the entire family usually worked together on the farm. In urban families, the father held a job while the mother was the homemaker. In both rural and urban families, the mother generally took care of the house and children, and divorce

10 was unusual.

    By World War II, the typical family had begun to change. Thousands of farm families had moved to the cities in search of jobs, and the nuclear family was becoming more common. Large numbers of women had begun to work outside the home, though most mothers continued to be housewives.

15   Since the 1960s, U.S. families have changed a great deal, partly because of the high divorce rate in America. Increasing economic pressures have also led to new variations on the American family. Today, in addition to traditional families, there are single-parent families, step or blended families (families where two people with children remarry), and families with young children

20 where both parents work full-time.

Understanding Vocabulary

1. What are extended family groups? What is the nuclear family?
2. Which word does *not* belong?

    a. typical   d. unusual

    b. average   e. common

    c. normal

3. Match the synonyms (words with similar meanings).

average	change
blended	typical
city	urban
housewife	homemaker
variation	mixed

Discussing Ideas

1. Is there one "typical" family type in the United States today? Was there in the past?
2. In your native country or culture, is there a "typical" family? If so, what is the typical family like?

PART ONE

Simple Present and Present Continuous Tenses

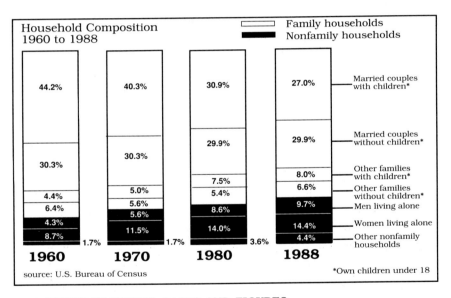

Household Composition 1960 to 1988

☐ Family households
■ Nonfamily households

1960	1970	1980	1988	
44.2%	40.3%	30.9%	27.0%	Married couples with children*
		29.9%	29.9%	Married couples without children*
30.3%	30.3%			
		7.5%	8.0%	Other families with children*
4.4%	5.0%	5.4%	6.6%	Other families without children*
6.4%	5.6%			
	5.6%	8.6%	9.7%	Men living alone
4.3%	11.5%	14.0%	14.4%	Women living alone
8.7%			4.4%	Other nonfamily households
1.7%	1.7%	3.6%		

source: U.S. Bureau of Census   *Own children under 18

THE AMERICAN FAMILY: FACTS AND FIGURES

Today the American family is steadily getting smaller, and "nonfamily" and single-parent households are increasing rapidly.

Fact: Almost one in four households consists of one person living alone.

Fact: Large families (six or more people) make up only 5 percent of American households.

Fact: Over 25 percent of American households include unrelated people.

Fact: One out of every four children—and over half of all black children—now has a single-parent home.

SIMPLE PRESENT TENSE

The simple present tense often refers to actions or situations that do not change frequently. It is used to describe habits or routines, to express opinions, or to make general statements of fact. The simple present can also be used to refer to the future.

Time expressions frequently used with this tense include *often, every day,* and *from time to time.* Questions with *When . . . ?* and *How often . . . ?* are also common with this tense.

Fact	Alan and Lu **are** married. They **have** two children. Both Alan and Lu **work.**
Routine	Lu **teaches** every day. She **doesn't get** home until 4:30.
Opinion	**Do** they **enjoy** their work? Lu **likes** her classes very much. Alan **isn't** happy with his job.
Reference to the future	Next month, Lu **has** vacation. She **doesn't teach** next month.

Note: See pages 254 and 255 for spelling rules for *-s* endings with *he, she,* and *it.* Remember that *-s* has three pronunciations: /ez/ after *-ch, -sh, -s, -x,* and *-z* endings; /s/ after voiceless endings; and /z/ after voiced endings.

/ez/   boxes, buzzes, kisses, watches, wishes
/s/   hits, hopes, laughs, looks
/z/   breathes, calls, listens, plays, stirs

■ **EXERCISE A**   Share some information about yourself and some opinions. Work with a classmate you don't know and ask each other these questions. Then try to add two or three original questions.

1. What is your name?
2. How old are you?
3. Where are you from?
4. What language(s) do you speak?
5. How many people are there in your family?
6. Do you live alone, with relatives, or with other people?
7. How do you like the city you live in? Is it very different from your hometown?

8. Do you have a job? If so, what is your job like?
9. Name two things you do every day. Name two things you don't do.
10. Name two things you like to do. Name two things you don't like to do.

■ **EXERCISE B** Form complete sentences from the following cues. Pay attention to the spelling and pronunciation of the *-s* endings.

Examples   be a full-time student
Fernando is a full-time student.
live alone
He lives alone.

1. get up very early on weekdays
2. leave for school at 7:45
3. have classes from 9:00 to 2:30
4. study at the library until 5:00
5. go home and watch the news
6. fix dinner and eat
7. do the laundry once a week
8. play tennis every weekend
9. worry about his future
10. enjoy life as a student

■ **YOUR TURN**   Tell your classmates a little more about your schedule. What is your typical schedule during the week? on weekends?

■ **EXERCISE C** The following gives you factual information about the average U.S. family today. Complete the sentences with the simple present forms (third person singular) of the verbs in parentheses. Pay attention to the spelling and pronunciation of the -s endings.

Example   In the United States today, the average female

*marries*_____ (marry) at age 23.8, and the average male

*gets*_____ (get) married at age 26.2.

1. The average family in the United States _____ (consist) of a mother, a father, and 1.6 children.

2. The U.S. government _____ (predict) that the average family will soon consist of only 2.3 people.

3. Over 25 percent of the U.S. population never _____ (marry).

4. The average family _____ (own) 1.5 cars and _____ (use) around a thousand gallons of gas per year.

5. One out of every two children under age six _____ (go) to a preschool.

6. One in four children _____ (live) in a single-parent home or _____ (stay) with relatives.

7. The average teenager _____ (watch) around twenty-eight hours of television every week.

8. One in four teenagers _____ (drop) out of high school.

9. A child with a working mother _____ (get) better grades, on average, than a child with a nonworking mother.

10. In general, a child in a small family _____ (finish) more years of education and _____ (end) up with a higher-paying job than a child in a large family.

■ **YOUR TURN** What information do you know about the average family in your culture? Share any factual information you know with your classmates.

Adverbs of Frequency and Other Time Expressions

Expressions such as the following are frequently used with the simple present tense. Many of these expressions also appear with verbs in the present and past perfect tenses.

ADVERBS OF FREQUENCY		OTHER TIME EXPRESSIONS
always	. . . 100 percent . . .	without fail
almost always		as a rule
usually, generally, typically, commonly, normally		on a regular basis
		by and large
often, frequently		in general
sometimes		at times, from time to time
occasionally		on occasion
seldom		(every) now and then
rarely		(every) now and again
hardly ever		once in a (great) while
almost never		
never	. . . 0 percent . . .	

Placement of Adverbs of Frequency

Adverbs of frequency generally come before the main verb in a sentence. They usually follow auxiliary verbs and *be* used as a main verb. *Ever,* meaning "at any time," is often used in questions and negatives. Longer time expressions are normally placed at the beginning or the end of a sentence.

In statements with one verb	We **usually** go to the movies on Mondays. We **almost always** eat dinner late. I **seldom** finish my work before 6:00.
In statements with auxiliary verbs and *be* as the main verb	Our classes are **generally** interesting. I don't **always** enjoy them, however. We have **occasionally** skipped classes.
In questions	Are you **ever** late for class? Do you **usually** get to class on time?
Longer expressions with verbs in all tenses	**As a rule,** we get to class early. I'm late **every now and then.**

■ **EXERCISE D** In pairs, take turns asking and answering these questions. Then add a few original questions. Give complete answers.

1. What is something that you always do every morning?
2. What is something that you never eat for breakfast?
3. What is something that you seldom wear?
4. Who is someone that you occasionally write to?
5. Who is someone that you hardly ever see now?
6. What is something that you generally do on weekends?

■ **EXERCISE E** Complete the passage with the simple present forms of the verbs in parentheses. Add adverbs when indicated.

A U.S. COMMUTER

Dave Peterson *generally wakes* _____ (wake / generally) up at 5:45 A.M., and he _____₁ (be / usually) ready for breakfast by 6:15. It _____₂ (take) him about ten minutes to have some coffee and a piece of toast. His children _____ _____₃ (be / always) up early too, but they _____ _____₄ (not leave) for school until 7:15, so the family _____ _____₅ (have / seldom) breakfast together.

   Dave _____₆ (run) out the door at 6:30 and _____₇ (have) just enough time to make the express train. He _____₈ (pick / always) up a copy of the *Wall Street Journal* near the station and _____₉ (fold) it neatly in quarters, lengthwise — ready for the train ride. Like Dave, thousands of commuters _____₁₀ (read) their neatly folded newspapers on the train each morning.

As a rule, Dave _____₁₁ (arrive) at the office a few minutes before 8:30. Most of his coworkers _____₁₂ (get / rarely) there before 9:00. Dave _____₁₃ (not have) to be in until 9:00 either, but it _____₁₄ (look / always) good to be at work early.

Five days a week, forty-nine weeks a year, Dave's mornings _____₁₅ (begin) like that, just like clockwork.

■ **YOUR TURN** How does your father's or mother's day usually begin? How does your husband's or your wife's? Choose a family member and tell or write about a typical weekday or weekend morning in his or her life.

PRESENT CONTINUOUS TENSE

The present continuous tense describes activities that are happening right now and current activities of a general nature. In some cases, it can also refer to the future. As a rule, the present continuous tense is used for activities that are temporary rather than permanent.

Time expressions frequently used with this tense include *now, at the moment, still, today, nowadays, these days,* and expressions with *this* (*this morning, this quarter, this year*).

Activities at the moment of speaking	John **is reading** the newspaper now. The children **are playing** with their toys. I**'m cooking** dinner.
Current activities	Sandy and Jim **are raising** two children. They**'re working** very hard.
Reference to the future	They**'re not traveling** to Europe this summer. They**'re taking** the children to Disneyland instead.

Note: See pages 254 and 255 for spelling rules for verbs ending in *-ing.*

■ **EXERCISE F** Work with a new partner and ask each other these questions. Answer in complete sentences using the present continuous tense.

1. What are three things you are doing right now?
2. What are three things you are not doing right now?
3. What are two things that you are doing this quarter (semester)?
4. What are two things that you aren't doing?

■ **EXERCISE G** Use the present continuous tense to complete the following sentences. Pay attention to the spelling of the *-ing* endings.

1. Today many changes _are occurring_____ (occur) in attitudes toward and numbers of adoptions.

2. Couples and single people throughout the United States _____ _____ (choose) to adopt children.

3. Currently about two million couples _____ (try) to adopt children.

4. International adoption agencies _____ (place) many children from other countries in American homes.

5. Also, more and more couples _____ (begin) to adopt children (either American or foreign) with physical and/or mental handicaps.

VERBS NOT GENERALLY USED
IN THE CONTINUOUS TENSES

Certain types of verbs are seldom used in the continuous tenses, *except* in idiomatic uses or in descriptions of a definite action.

Feelings or Thoughts

These verbs are rarely used in a continuous tense; the verbs with an asterisk (*), however, sometimes appear in the present perfect continuous. The verbs *think* and *consider* occasionally appear in the present continuous.

FEELING OR THOUGHT	SPECIFIC ACTIVITY	VERBS	
We **don't consider** this a problem. I **don't think** this is a good idea. What **does** this **mean**?	We **have been considering** several other possibilities. I **am thinking** about another possibility now. I **have been meaning** to talk with you about that.	appreciate be believe consider* dislike hate know like love mean*	mind miss need prefer recognize remember think* understand want*

Perceptions

These verbs sometimes appear in a continuous tense in the description of a specific action or in certain idioms.

PERCEPTION	ACTION	VERBS	
This apple **looks** good. It **tastes** delicious.	I **am looking at** the apple now. I **am tasting** the apple now.	appear hear* look see*	seem smell sound taste

⟶

Possession

These verbs almost never appear in continuous tenses, except for the verb *have*. In idiomatic use, *be having* has several meanings, including "be experiencing" or "be eating, drinking."

POSSESSION	ACTION	VERBS
We **own** a car. It **belongs to** my brother and me. He **has** the car today.	My brother **is having** a great time with our new car. My brother and I **are having** dinner together tonight.	belong to cost have* own possess

■ **EXERCISE H Contrast of Present Tenses** Complete the passage with appropriate forms of the verbs in parentheses. Add adverbs when indicated.

FAMILY RESPONSIBILITIES

Household chores _are usually_ (be / usually) boring. All of us in the Peterson household _____ *have* _____₁ (have) busy schedules, so we _____ *try* _____₂ (try) to share the chores. Our plan _____ *seldom works* _____₃ (work / seldom) out though! For example, our sons, Dan and Ed, _____ *usually do* _____₄ (do / usually) the dinner dishes, but tonight they _____ *are studying* _____₅ (study) for exams. So guess who _____ *is washing* _____₆ (wash) the dishes tonight? Me! Our daughter, Sue, _____ *normally takes*_____₇ (take / normally) care of the laundry, but she _____ *is visiting* _____₈ (visit) friends out of town. So guess who _____ *is doing* _____₉ (do) the laundry this week? Me! My husband and I _____ *alternate* _____₁₀ (alternate) cooking, as a rule, but he _____ *is meeting* _____₁₁ (meet) with one of his most important clients this evening. So guess who _____ *is making* _____₁₂ (make) dinner again? Me!

I _____don't mind_____ 13 (not mind) doing all these chores, and, in fact, I _____even like_____ 14 (like / even) housework. Time _____is always_____ 15 (be / always) my problem, however. I _____work_____ 16 (work) thirty-five hours a week, and I _____often have_____ 17 (have / often) to stay late at my job. I _____understand_____ 18 (understand) that the family schedules _____change_____ 19 (change) and that "someone" _____needs_____ 20 (need) to keep up the house. But I _____almost always_____ 21 (seem / almost always) to be the "someone." It _____is not_____ 22 (not be) easy to have two full-time jobs!

■ **YOUR TURN** Who usually does the cooking at your house? Who is cooking tonight? Who usually does the cleaning? Who is doing the cleaning this week?

PART TWO

Simple Past and Past Continuous Tenses, *When* and *While*

THE "TRADITIONAL" FAMILY

In the "traditional" family of the past, the father had a job, the mother kept house, and the children were always perfect. Or, at least, that is our image of the traditional family!

SIMPLE PAST TENSE

The simple past tense describes actions or situations that began and ended in the past. Time expressions frequently used with this tense include *ago* (*two weeks ago, a month ago today*), *the day before yesterday, in the past,* and *in 1991* (*in March, in spring,* etc.). Sequence expressions are also used: *first, then, later, finally,* and *last.*

| **Actions and situations that began and ended in the past** | Six years ago, we **bought** a house in the suburbs.
Then we **found** an apartment in the city.
We finally **moved** into our apartment last year.
We never **liked** life in the suburbs. |

Note: See pages 256–259 for a list of irregular past forms. See pages 254 and 255 for spelling rules for regular *-ed* endings. Remember that *-ed* has three pronunciations: /ed/ after *d* and *t* endings, /t/ after voiceless endings, and /d/ after voiced endings.

    /ed/   insisted, needed, waded, wanted
    /t/   boxed, hoped, kissed, laughed, looked, washed, watched
    /d/   breathed, called, listened, nudged, played, stirred

■ **EXERCISE A**   **Spelling and Pronunciation Review** This exercise tells the story of one mother. Using the simple past tense of these regular verbs, form complete sentences from the cues below. Pay attention to the spelling and pronunciation of the *-ed* endings.

Example   work hard all her life
Mother worked hard all her life.

1. start her day very early
2. serve breakfast
3. wash the dishes
4. fold and iron the laundry
5. fix lunch
6. shop for groceries
7. cook dinner
8. never permit us to watch TV on school nights
9. study with us, play with us, laugh with us, and cry with us
10. listen to our problems
11. always worry about us
12. want us to be happy

■ **EXERCISE B   Spelling Review** This exercise tells the story of one father. Using the simple past tense of these irregular verbs, form sentences from the cues below. Pay attention to the spellings of the irregular forms.

Example   be a kind man
Father was a kind man.

1. wake up early
2. take a shower
3. get dressed
4. always wear a dark suit and a white shirt
5. eat breakfast slowly
6. read the newspaper carefully
7. usually ride the train to work
8. sometimes drive to work
9. come home at 6:30 or 7:00
10. have dinner late
11. sit in his armchair and light his pipe
12. always tell us stories at night

■ **EXERCISE C** This exercise tells about growing up in a more traditional society. Make negative statements from the cues below.

Example   not have as much freedom as they have now
**Years ago, young people did not have as much freedom
as they have now.**

1. not be as free as they are today
2. not have cars
3. not stay out late
4. not date until the end of high school
5. not move away from home immediately after high school
6. not always make their own choices

■ **EXERCISE D** In pairs, take turns asking and answering these questions about your families. Then try to add some original questions.

1. Where did you grow up?
2. What was your mother like? What was your father like?
3. Did your mother do the cooking? Did your father cook too?
4. Who did the cleaning?
5. Did you help around the house? Did your brothers and sisters help?
6. What was your neighborhood like? Were there many children nearby?

■ **EXERCISE E** Complete the passage with the simple past forms of the verbs in parentheses.

THE "AMERICAN DREAM"

The "American dream" is an idea that _grew_____ (grow) from TV programs, books, and stories about family life. The idea _____₁ (begin) in the 1950s, after World War II. What _____₂ (be) the "dream"?

As the first step, families _____₃ (buy) or _____₄ (build) a cozy little home in the suburbs. This _____₅ (mean / often) a long commute to work. Many husbands _____₆ (ride) the train or _____₇ (drive) two hours each way, but this _____₈ (be) part of the dream.

The husband "_____₉ (wear) the pants" in the family. He _____₁₀ (make) the decisions because he _____₁₁ (go) to work, he _____₁₂ (pay) the bills, and he "_____"₁₃ (put) food on the table. Of course, *his wife* actually _____₁₄ (cook) the meals!

The wife _____₁₅ (spend) her time at home. She _____₁₆ (take) care of the children and _____₁₇ (keep) house. Occasionally she _____₁₈ (find) time for a hobby.

According to the dream, everyone _____₁₉ (be) happy with this arrangement. This _____₂₀ (be) the image that people _____₂₁ (hold) of the "perfect family." If the husband or wife _____₂₂ (feel) bored or discontented, he or she _____₂₃ (hide) these feelings.

1950   **1990**

■ **YOUR TURN** In your society, what is the image of the "perfect family"? Does it really exist? Give a brief description of it and then compare this image to your view of what actually exists in your society.

_____

_____

_____

_____

_____

_____

PAST CONTINUOUS TENSE

The past continuous tense describes actions in progress in the recent past or at a specific time in the past. It is often used to describe or "set" a scene. The following time expressions are frequently used with this tense: *a few minutes (moments) ago, at that time, then, just,* and *still.*

Events in the recent past	Mary, we **were** just **looking** for you. Oh! I **was taking** a short nap.
Events at a specific time in the past	A year ago, we **were living** in the Back Bay. At that time, I **was** still **working** at the bank, and my wife **was taking** classes.
Description of a scene	It was a beautiful summer evening. We **were** all **sitting** and **talking** on the front porch. Dad **was playing** the guitar, the boys **were singing**, and I **was watching** the stars.

Note: See pages 11 and 12 for a list of verbs not generally used in the continuous tenses. See pages 254 and 255 for spelling rules for verbs with *-ing* endings.

■ **EXERCISE F** Use the past continuous tense to answer the following questions in complete sentences.

1. What were you doing two hours ago?
2. Where were you living a year ago?
3. What were you doing when you decided to come to this school?
4. What were you thinking about a moment ago?
5. What was your classmate, _____, doing a few minutes ago?
6. What were you doing the day before yesterday?
7. What was your teacher doing at this time yesterday?
8. What were you studying two weeks ago?

■ **EXERCISE G** These passages describe scenes from the past. Complete them with the past continuous forms of the verbs in parentheses. Pay attention to the spelling of the *-ing* endings.

1. I have a special memory of Christmas when I was five years old. My aunts, uncles, and cousins _were visiting_____ (visit) us. I _____ (wear) my beautiful new red dress. We _____ (sit) around the Christmas tree, and everyone _____ (open) Christmas presents. I _____ (watch) one big present near the corner of the room. Then my mother took me over to that present. It was for me! It was the most beautiful dollhouse I had ever seen!

2. I have a special childhood memory of a summer night when I was seven or eight. My mom and dad and my sisters _____₁ (sit) on the front porch. The sun _____₂ (set), and the sky _____₃ (become) red and golden. My sisters _____₄ (swing) on the porch swing, and my mother _____₅ (rock) in her rocking chair. Our dog _____₆ (lie) on the steps. My father _____₇ (play) his guitar and _____₈ (sing). Everyone _____₉ (listen) to him. He loved to sing, and he had a wonderful voice. I felt so happy and peaceful and secure. That night is one of my best memories.

WHEN AND WHILE

When and *while* are frequently used to connect two past actions. Chapter 6 includes more information on these connecting words.

while	He was watching TV **while** I was doing the dishes.	*While* may connect two past continuous actions that were occurring at the same time.
when or **while**	John was talking to the man at the door **when** his mother phoned. **While** John was talking to the man at the door, his mother phoned.	*When* or *while* may connect a simple past and past continuous action—*while* + the action in progress or *when* + the action that interrupted it.
when	**When** the doorbell rang, John answered it.	*When* may connect two simple past actions; *when* comes before the action that happened first.

■ **EXERCISE H**   Complete the passages with the simple past or past continuous forms of the verbs in parentheses.

This morning everything went wrong at the Peterson household.

1. I _wanted_____ (want) to get up early this morning, but

   I _____₁ (forget) to set the alarm. So I

_____₂ (oversleep). When I _____₃
(get) up, my brother _____₄ (take) a long
shower. So I _____₅ (have) to wait for a long time.
While I _____₆ (ride) my bike to school, I
_____₇ (get) a flat tire. I _____₈
(miss) my first class, and I _____₉ (be) late for my
second class. It _____₁₀ (not be) a good morning.

2. I _____₁ (wake) up very early this morning and
_____₂ (leave) the house while everyone else
_____₃ (sleep / still). I _____₄
(catch) the bus at 6:45 in order to get to work early. I
_____₅ (read) the newspaper on the bus, and I
_____₆ (not pay) attention to the traffic when
suddenly a car "_____₇" (run) a red light and
_____₈ (hit) the bus on my side. When the car
_____₉ (crash) into us, I _____₁₀
(fall) off my seat, _____₁₁ (cut) my head, and
_____₁₂ (break) my arm. What a day!

■ **EXERCISE I** Using the simple past and past continuous tenses with *when* and *while*, tell a story using the following information.

Example This morning everything went wrong for Dave Peterson too. **At 8:35 A.M., Dave woke up late and took a two-minute shower. While he was getting out of the shower, . . .**

8:35 A.M.	wakes up late
8:36 – 8:38 A.M.	takes a shower
8:39 A.M.	gets out of the shower
8:39 A.M.	falls on the floor
8:39 – 8:40 A.M.	shaves
8:40 A.M.	cuts his face
8:40 A.M.	throws the razor on the floor
8:41 – 8:42 A.M.	gets dressed
8:42 A.M.	tears a hole in his shirt
8:43 A.M.	finds a new shirt
8:44 A.M.	makes coffee
8:45 A.M.	pours the coffee
8:45 A.M.	spills coffee on his shirt
8:46 – 8:47 A.M.	looks for another clean shirt
8:47 A.M.	hears the doorbell
8:47 A.M.	runs to the door, but no one is there
8:48 A.M.	loses his temper
8:48 A.M.	goes back to the bedroom
8:50 A.M.	lies down and goes back to sleep

PART THREE

Future Tenses, *Be Going to*

NEW DIRECTIONS IN FAMILY LIFE

What is family life going to be like in the next century? Social scientists are making these predictions.

Prediction: Nine out of ten Americans will marry, but they will get married later than past generations did.

Prediction: Most couples will have children, but they will have fewer children and have them later in life.

Prediction: The divorce rate will remain high, but most who divorce will be remarrying within a year or two of the divorce.

SIMPLE FUTURE TENSE

The simple future tense expresses intentions, and it can be used to express offers, promises, predictions, and requests.

Time expressions such as the following are often used with future forms: *this afternoon (evening), tonight, later, in a while, in the future, in September,* and *in 2025.*

Intentions	I'll **try** to be home early tonight.
Offers and Promises	I'll **help** you with the housework in a little while. Thanks. Then I **will make** you a special dinner!
Predictions	With your help, we'll **finish** by ten o'clock.
Requests	**Will** you **promise** to help?

Other Forms Used for the Future

Be going to	I'm **going to be** home no later than 7:00. What **are** we **going to have** for dinner?	*Going to* is often used to express specific future plans. It is used frequently in conversation and is often pronounced /gonna/ or /gunna/.
Present continuous	I **am serving** dinner at 7:30. The guests **are coming** around 7:00.	Both the present continuous and the simple present can be used to express future time. Generally a time expression or the context indicates that the action or situation is in the future. Verbs such as *go, come, arrive,* and *leave* are often used in present tenses even when they have future meanings.
Simple present	Dinner **is** at 7:30. We **leave** for the movie at 9:00.	

■ **EXERCISE A** In pairs, take turns asking and answering the following questions.

1. Will you see your family (boyfriend, girlfriend, best friend) soon?
2. When are you going to call them (him, her) next?
3. Will the call be long-distance?
4. Will it be expensive?
5. When are you going to write your next letter to your family (boyfriend, girlfriend, and so on)?
6. Is anyone coming to visit you soon?
7. When do the guests arrive?
8. What are you planning to do with them?

■ **EXERCISE B** Complete the passage with the simple present, *be going to,* or the simple future form of the verbs in parentheses. In some cases, more than one choice may be possible. Be prepared to discuss your choices.

THE HIGH COST OF CHILDREN

According to Lawrence Olson in his book *Costs of Children*, in the future, children _will become_ (become) much more expensive to raise. American parents of children born in the 1980s _____ _____₁ (spend), on an average, $226,000 to raise a firstborn son to age twenty-two. A firstborn daughter _____₂ (be) even more expensive—$247,000. These figures _____ _____₃ (not take) inflation into account, however.

Olson _____₄ (estimate) that it _____ _____₅ (cost) approximately 2.2 percent more to raise a girl than a boy. He _____₆ (say) the difference is because of such items as wedding expenses, cosmetics, and transportation. Olson _____₇ (base) the total figures on the assumption that a child of either sex _____₈ (attend) a private college or university for four years.

FUTURE CONTINUOUS TENSE

The future continuous tense generally refers to actions that will be in progress, often at a specified time, in the future. These time expressions are often used with the future continuous tense: *at this time next week* (*month, year,* etc.), *at that time* (*at 3:00, 4:00,* etc.), *the day after tomorrow,* and *a week* (*year, month*) *from today.*

Actions in progress in the future	Can you imagine! At this time tomorrow, we'll **be landing** in London! Yes, but at the same time next week, we'll **be flying** home.

Note: See pages 11 and 12 for a list of verbs not generally used in the continuous tenses. See pages 254 and 255 for spelling rules for verbs with *-ing* endings.

■ **EXERCISE C**   Complete the following in your own words, using the future continuous.

Example   Right now I am sitting in class. At this time tomorrow, . . .
I'll be studying at the library.

1. Right now I am living _____ (with my parents / in an apartment). A month from now, . . .
2. This session I am going to _____ (name of school). Next session . . .
3. This session I am taking English. Next session . . .
4. Right now I am studying grammar. At this time tomorrow, . . .

■ **EXERCISE D**   In pairs, take turns asking and answering the following questions.

Example   What will you be doing the day after tomorrow?
I will probably be studying for a test.

1. What will you be doing at this time on Saturday?
2. What will you be studying a month from now?
3. Will you still be going to school six months from now?
4. Will you be working a year from now?
5. Where will you be living at that time?
6. Will you be using English then?

■ **EXERCISE E** **Contrast of Present and Future Tenses** Complete the passage with appropriate present or future forms of the verbs in parentheses. Several choices may be possible. Be prepared to explain your choices.

AN OLDER U.S. POPULATION

Americans now in their forties *will most likely live* (live / most likely) to be at least eighty, and people now in their thirties _____₁ (live) even longer. Some population scientists _____₂ (predict), in fact, that healthy, active lifetimes past 100 years _____₃ (seem / not) unusual for many of today's infants.

Population experts _____₄ (estimate) that in 2050 the median age in the United States _____₅ (reach) approximately forty-two years. They also _____₆ (estimate) that more than 20 percent of the people alive in 2050 _____₇ (be) older than sixty-five. Moreover, the majority of the population in 2050 _____₈ (consist) of people much older than what we _____₉ (consider / now) middle age.

These population changes _____₁₀ (cause) tremendous changes in future attitudes. By then, we _____₁₁ (call) twenty-year-olds "youngsters," almost babies! At forty-five, people _____₁₂ (come / just) into their prime, while at sixty-five, people _____₁₃ (enter) "middle age." Perhaps within our lifetimes, a person _____₁₄ (not be) "elderly" until after his or her hundredth birthday!

PART FOUR

Present Perfect Continuous and Present Perfect Tenses

CHANGING ROLES

The traditional roles of men and women have changed a great deal, and these changes have affected American society dramatically. Since the beginning of the 1960s, more and more women have been entering the work force. And men have been getting much more involved in the daily life of the family.

PRESENT PERFECT CONTINUOUS TENSE

The present perfect continuous tense describes actions or situations that began in the past and have continued to the moment of speaking. This tense often implies that the action or situation will continue in the future. With time expressions such as the following, this tense stresses the duration of an activity: *for* + period of time, *since* + beginning time, and *all morning* (*day, week,* etc.). Other expressions include *lately, so far, till now, to date, up to now, until now,* and questions with *How long . . . ?*

Actions and situations that began in the past and have continued to the present	How long **has** Martin **been talking** on the phone? He**'s been talking** for nearly two hours! Lately he and his girlfriend **have been calling** each other every night.

Note: See pages 254 and 255 for spelling rules for verbs ending in *-ing*. See pages 11 and 12 for a list of verbs not generally used in the continuous tenses.

■ **EXERCISE A** In pairs, take turns asking and answering questions. Using the cues below, form questions with *How long . . . ?* and answers with *for, since,* or *all.* You may give long or short answers.

Example   clean the house / early this morning
> STUDENT A: **You look tired! How long have you been cleaning the house?**
> STUDENT B: **Too long! I've been cleaning it since early this morning.**
> or
> **Too long! Since early this morning.**

1. wash dishes / 9:00
2. do laundry / 7:30 in the morning
3. iron / over two hours
4. shop for school clothes / afternoon
5. try to put the baby to sleep / 8:00 P.M.

PRESENT PERFECT TENSE (1)

In some cases, the present perfect tense, like the present perfect continuous tense, can also describe actions or situations that developed in the past and that have continued up until the moment of speaking. It implies that the action or situation will continue in the future. A time expression, such as those given below, is used to give this meaning with verbs such as *begin, expect, hope, live, study, teach, wait,* and *work.* In addition, this use of the present perfect tense occurs frequently with verbs not generally used in the continuous tenses.* Time expressions that give this meaning of the present perfect tense include *for, since, so far, to date, till now,* and *up to now.*

With *for, since,* and other time expressions	Jack **has worked** very hard for several weeks. He**'s studied** a lot since the beginning of school. Up to now, his teacher **has expected** a lot. His teacher **hasn't taught** accounting for very long.
With verbs not generally used in the continuous tenses*	He **hasn't understood** everything in class. The class **has seemed** difficult. The homework **has been** hard.

Note: See pages 254 and 255 for spelling rules for verbs ending in *-ed.* See pages 256–259 for a list of irregular past participles.

---

* Remember that the following nonaction verbs are occasionally used in the present perfect continuous: *consider, mean, think, want.* See pages 11 and 12.

■ **EXERCISE B** Answer the following questions in your own words. Use *for, since,* or other time expressions in your answers.

1. How long have you been in this country?
2. How long have you lived in this city?
3. How long have you studied English?
4. Have you understood everything in your classes so far?
5. Up to now, which class has seemed the most difficult?

■ **EXERCISE C** Complete the following with present perfect or present perfect continuous forms of the verbs in parentheses. Use contractions when possible. Mark all cases where both forms are possible and try to explain any difference in meaning between the two tenses.

Dear Alex,

I _'ve meant (I've been meaning)_ (mean) to write you for weeks, but I _____1 (not have) much time. I _____2 (be) incredibly busy. My life _____3 (seem) much more difficult during the last few months, and I _____4 (not be) able to do anything but work and help at home. I _____5 (enjoy / really) fatherhood and the new baby, and I _____6 (not mind) all the work. But, to be honest, I _____7 (feel) *so* tired! Our neighbors _____8 (give) us some help, and we _____9 (appreciate / really) that! We _____10 (consider) looking for extra help, but we _____11 (not decide) about that yet.

It's funny. Until now, I _____12 (hate / always) cooking, but since we had the baby, I _____13 (cook) dinner almost every night, and I _____14 (begin) to like it! The dinners _____15 (not be) perfect, but at least we eat. And, because of the baby, I _____16 (learn) so many new things about life — like how to change a diaper!

Along other lines, everything _____17 (be) fine here. And, how _____18 you _____19 (do)? How _____20 things _____21 (go)? I _____22 (think) of you a lot. Please give my best to everyone.

Love,
Alfonso

PRESENT PERFECT TENSE (2)

The present perfect tense can have a past-to-present time frame. It has a more common use, however. The present perfect tense frequently refers to an event that happened (or did not happen) at an unknown or unspecified time in the past. It also refers to *repeated* past actions. *No specific time* is given with these statements. When a specific past time is used, the verb is in the past tense.

Time expressions frequently used with this meaning of the present perfect tense include *already, ever, recently, still, yet*, and (*how*) *many times*.

Events at an unspecified time in the past	**Have** you ever **gone** to Austria? I **haven't** (ever) **been** there. I**'ve visited** my relatives in Germany though. I went there last year.
Repeated actions at unspecified times in the past	I**'ve been** to Europe five times. We**'ve called** there several times this month. How many times **have** you **visited** your sister in Germany? We **haven't gone** there very often. We visited her in 1985 and in 1989.

Note: See pages 256–259 for a list of irregular past participles and pages 254 and 255 for spelling rules for the *-ed* ending of regular past participles.

■ **EXERCISE D** The following sentences use the present perfect tense. Tell which actions or situations are still true now and which occurred at an unspecified time in the past.

Examples Sally has worked at that hospital. **(unspecified time in the past)**
Sally has worked at that hospital since 1987. **(still true)**

1. Sally has held a job at the hospital for several years.
2. Lately her work has been very stressful.
3. The stress has affected her.
4. Sally has changed a great deal.
5. She has looked for other jobs.
6. Sally has always worked because she has needed the money.
7. She has considered going back to school.
8. I've meant to call her since I learned about her problems.

Already, (Not) Ever, Just, Never, Recently, Still, and *(Not) Yet*

These adverbs are frequently used with the present perfect tense.

Questions	Have you **ever** read that book?	*Ever* must come before the past participle.
	Have you **already** read the book? Have you read it **already**? Have you read it **yet**?	*Already* may be used before the past participle or at the end of the sentence. *Yet* is generally used at the end of the sentence.
Affirmative statements	I've **already** read it. I've **just** read it. I've read it **recently**. I've **recently** read it.	*Already* and *just* come before the past participle. *Recently* may come at the end of the sentence or before the past participle. It is sometimes used to begin the sentence.
Negative statements	I have **never** read it. I have**n't ever** read it. I **still** haven't read it. I haven't read it **yet**.	*Never* generally comes before the past participle. *Not ever* must come before the past participle. *Still* must come before *have* or *has*. *Yet* is generally used at the end of the sentence.

■ **EXERCISE E** In pairs, take turns asking and answering questions about family responsibilities. Use *Have you ever . . . ?* and *How many times have you . . . ?* with the following information. Then try to add two or three questions of your own.

Example   take care of a baby
        STUDENT A: **Have you ever taken care of a baby?**
        STUDENT B: **Yes, I have. I have two younger brothers.**

1. change a diaper
2. prepare a meal for your family
3. help children with their homework
4. do the laundry for your family
5. read stories to children
6. help take care of an older person

■ **EXERCISE F** In pairs, take turns making statements and responses. Complete each conversation by adding a sentence that uses *already*.

Example   STUDENT A: Don't start the washing machine! I haven't put all my clothes in yet!
    STUDENT B: **Sorry! I've already started it.**

1. Don't put the broom away. I haven't swept the floor yet.
   Sorry! . . .

2. Don't wax the floor. I haven't washed it yet.
   Sorry! . . .

3. Don't walk in the kitchen. The floor hasn't dried yet.
   Sorry! . . .

4. Don't mail those bills! I haven't signed the checks yet.
   Sorry! . . .

5. Don't throw the newspaper away! Your father hasn't read it yet.
   Sorry! . . .

■ **EXERCISE G** In pairs, take turns making statements and responses. Complete each conversation by forming sentences with the verbs in parentheses and *not . . . yet*.

Example   STUDENT A: This chicken is terrific.
    STUDENT B: Oh, really? _____ (taste)
    I haven't tasted it yet.

1. These cookies are delicious!

   Oh, really? _____ (try)

2. The vegetables are tasteless.

   I know. _____ (salt)

3. The Lords are here.

   Oh, really? _____ (talk)

4. Melanie looks terrific!

   Oh, really? _____ (see)

5. Bill Lord is a wonderful person.

   Oh, really? _____ (meet)

■ **EXERCISE H**   In pairs, take turns asking and answering the following questions. Complete each conversation by forming sentences with the information in parentheses and *still . . . not.*

Example   STUDENT A: Have you studied all the chapters for the test yet?
              STUDENT B: Yes, but _____ . (review my notes)
              Yes, but I still haven't reviewed my notes.

1. Have Nancy and Jerry bought a new house yet?

   Yes, but _____ . (sell the old one)

2. Has Gary finished painting his house yet?

   Yes, but _____ . (repair the roof)

3. Has Melanie put in the vegetable garden yet?

   Yes, but _____ . (plant the flowers)

4. Have they had their computer for a while?

   Yes, but _____ . (learn how to program it)

5. Has Tim's baby, Alice, started walking yet?

   Yes, but _____ . (begin talking)

■ **YOUR TURN** Have you written to your family lately? Have you been to the language lab? Have you done your laundry? Have you paid your rent? List four things that you planned to do but still haven't done.

■ **EXERCISE I Contrast of Tenses** Complete the passage with present perfect, present perfect continuous, or simple past forms of the verbs in parentheses. Mark any cases where more than one tense is possible and be prepared to explain any difference in meaning between the tenses.

GROWING OLD IN AMERICA

For years, the elderly *were* _____ (be) the "forgotten" members of American society, but in recent times, this _____1 (change). The elderly _____2 (begin) to form groups such as the Gray Panthers to represent their rights and their interests. These groups _____3 (affect) America politically, economically, and psychologically. Above all, they _____4 (remind) America that elderly people are valuable and energetic citizens.

Today's elderly are active in all aspects of American society, especially in the work force. Many older people _____5 (choose) to return to work after their retirement. According to supermarket manager Arlo Fitzpatrick, who _____6 (hire / already) eight people over sixty-five as cashiers and baggers, "Senior citizens are reliable and hardworking. Perhaps that's because they _____7 (be) through more. They _____8 (experience) the bad as well as the good in life, and they _____9 (learn) a lot of lessons that younger people _____10 (not learn / yet). My senior citizens work harder than many employees half their age."

The elderly _____11 (contribute) much to America, and they will continue to do so. As sixty-seven-year-old Dorothy Jackson _____12 (say), "Age is only a state of mind. Just because you _____13 (grow) old does not mean that your time to enjoy life, to be productive, to grow and learn _____14 (end)."

PART FIVE

Used to, Would, Was/Were Going to; Past Perfect Tense

THE OLD DAYS

"My pa used to play the violin. All of us children would gather around the potbellied stove, and we would be glued to the sounds of that old violin. Around 1950, after Pa had died, I tried to learn to play it. Others would pick it up from time to time. But in all these years nobody has made it 'sing' the way Pa used to."

— Al Monom, age 87, Middleton, Wisconsin

HABITUAL PAST — *USED TO* AND *WOULD*

Both *used to* + simple form and *would* + simple form are used to describe actions in the past that were repeated on a regular basis. For situations and continuous actions in the past, however, only *used to* is possible.

Repeated actions in the past	When I was a child, my family **would travel** in the West every summer. We **used to visit** the Grand Teton Mountains every year.
Continuous actions or situations in the past	My father **used to live** near the mountains. (not *would live*) He **used to work** in a national park. (not *would work*)
Past actions or situations that no longer exist	Campsites **used to be** free; now you have to pay to camp. (not *would be*)

Note: Do not confuse the constructions *used to* + simple form and *be used to* + gerund, which means "be accustomed to." Compare: *I used to get up early.* (*I don't anymore.*) *I am used to getting up early.* (*I frequently get up early, and it doesn't bother me.*)

■ **EXERCISE A** Using *would* or *used to*, change the following sentences from the simple past tense to the habitual past. Note any cases where *would* cannot be used.

Example   We lived in a small town.
  We used to live in a small town. (*Would* is not possible.)

1. Our family had a television, but we seldom watched it.
2. We always found other ways to pass the time.
3. All the children in the neighborhood were friends.
4. In the summer, we always played games, rode our bicycles, and went swimming.
5. All of us liked to swim.
6. In autumn, we always made big piles of leaves to jump in.
7. In winter, we skated and skied all the time.
8. Finally springtime came after months of winter.

■ **EXERCISE B** Using *used to* and adding *not anymore*, show a change in situation or habits from the past to the present.

Example   My cousin lived in Hawaii.
  My cousin used to live in Hawaii, but he doesn't anymore.

1. He went to college in Hawaii.
2. He cut classes often.
3. He swam in the ocean every day.
4. He had fun all the time.
5. He always got a good suntan.
6. He also failed all of his exams.

FUTURE IN THE PAST—*WAS/WERE GOING TO*

Was/were going to + verb is used to describe past intentions. In many cases, the intention was not completed.

Past intentions	Last summer, our family **was going to visit** friends in Colorado.
Past intentions that were not completed	Last summer, we **were going to visit** friends in Colorado, but we didn't have enough time. (Last summer, we *visited* friends there. = completed action)

■ **EXERCISE C**   In pairs, use these cues to ask and answer questions.

Example   clean your room
Have you cleaned your room yet?
I was going to clean it a while ago, but I didn't have time.

1. make your bed
2. sweep the floor
3. take the garbage out

4. pick your clothes up
5. do the laundry
6. iron your shirts

■ **YOUR TURN**   Have you made plans recently that did not work out? Were you going to take a trip? buy a car? write your family? Give at least four sentences about something that you were going to do yesterday (last week, last month, etc.) but haven't done yet.

■ **EXERCISE D**   Complete the following with past or present forms of *be going to*.

1. When I was a child, I dreamed I _____ (become) an astro-

   naut. I _____ (pilot) the first spaceship to Mars, and I

   _____ (make) history! Dreams change though. Next week I

   _____ (begin) working as an accountant.

2. When we were children, we dreamed that we _____ (be)

   famous scientists. And then we dreamed that we _____

   (become) famous movie stars. And then we _____ (get)

   jobs as pilots. We _____ (travel) all over the world! Dreams

   change though. Betty _____ (finish) law school soon, and

   I _____ (teach) English!

■ **YOUR TURN**   What did you dream that you were going to be? Do you still have the same dream?

PAST PERFECT TENSE

The past perfect tense refers to an activity or situation completed *before* another event or time in the past. This tense may be used in a simple sentence, but it generally contrasts with the simple past in a compound or complex sentence.

Time expressions such as *already, barely, just, no sooner, rarely, recently, still, yet, ever,* and *never,* or connecting words such as *after, before, by, by the time (that), until,* and *when* are often used with the past perfect. Chapter 6 includes more information on uses of this tense with connecting words and complex sentences.

Simple sentences	Until 1932, the O'Keefes **had lived** on a farm.
	By the end of 1932, they **had** already **lost** their farm and moved to the city.
Complex sentences	Before the Depression began, the O'Keefes **had been** prosperous farmers.
	The children **had** just **begun** school when their parents lost the farm.

Note: While the past perfect tense is often preferable in formal English, the simple past is frequently used instead of the past perfect in conversation. The meaning of the sentence must be clear, however. For example, in sentences with *when,* the time difference in the two tenses can change the meaning of the sentence.

Simple past + simple past	It **began** to rain when I **went** out.
	(The rain began at that time.)
Past perfect + simple past	It **had begun** to rain when I **went** out.
	(The rain had begun earlier.)

See pages 256–259 for a list of irregular past participles and pages 254 and 255 for spelling rules for the *-ed* ending.

■ **EXERCISE E**   This exercise tells the story of an immigrant family in the United States. Using *by* and the past perfect tense, form complete sentences from the cues below.

Example   1848 / John and Mary O'Keefe / leave Ireland
          By 1848, John and Mary O'Keefe had left Ireland.

1. 1850 / the O'Keefes / start a farm in Wisconsin
2. 1880s / the O'Keefes / raise a family of ten children
3. 1885 / their son John / marry Catherine
4. 1890 / Catherine / give birth to a daughter, Amanda
5. 1910 / Amanda / get married to Ed
6. 1920 / they / have a beautiful baby girl

■ **YOUR TURN** Do you know the story of your great-grandparents or your grandparents? Try to remember names and dates. Using *by* plus dates, briefly tell or write their story.

■ **EXERCISE F** Complete the following sentences by using either the simple past or the past perfect tense of the verbs in parentheses.

Example Before changing lifestyles *began*_____ (begin) to separate modern families, several generations of the same family *had often lived*_____ (live / often) together.

1. Until the automobile, the Depression, and the world wars

   _____ (bring) changes in U.S. society, American

   lifestyles _____ (remain) constant for a century.

2. American society _____ (begin / already) to

   change when World War II _____ (break out).

3. After rural families _____ (move) to the cities in

   search of work, they _____ (create) new lives

   there instead of returning to their farms.

4. Women _____ (work / rarely) outside the home

   before World War II _____ (produce) a labor

   shortage.

5. After women _____ (experience) the world of

   work, many _____ (find) it difficult to return to

   their traditional roles.

6. By the time World War II _____ (come) to an

   end, the American way of life _____ (change) tremen-

   dously.

■ **EXERCISE G Review of Tenses** Complete the following passage using appropriate forms of the verbs in parentheses. In some cases, more than one choice may be possible. Be prepared to discuss your choices.

THE NEW FATHERHOOD

Steve _played_ (play) in a high-school rock band and _____ 1 (do) long-distance bicycling during college, but in recent years, he _____ 2 (find) a new pastime in his children, Molly and Max. He not only _____ 3 (bathe), _____ 4 (change), and _____ 5 (feed) them but also gladly _____ 6 (take) the children on his fishing trips. Steve _____ 7 (view) his role in the practical aspects of baby care as typical of today's fathers: "Yesterday three other teachers and I _____ 8 (sit) in the office at school. We _____ 9 (talk) about our children and cloth versus disposable diapers!"

Since the 1950s and 1960s, tremendous changes _____ 10 (occur) in the roles that fathers _____ 11 (play), especially in the early years of their children's care. Steve _____ 12 (feel) that it _____ 13 (be) more important for him to share in the raising of Molly and Max than it _____ 14 (be) to earn a little more money each year. He _____ 15 (want / not) to be a stranger to his own children.

Fathers _____ 16 (appear) to have far more capacity to care for small children than people _____ 17 (think) in times past. In the past, psychologists _____ 18 (assume) that the mother _____ 19 (be) the better-suited parent for early childcare —both temperamentally and biologically. But recent research _____ 20 (suggest) that, given a chance, fathers _____ 21 (be) as caring as mothers with their young children.

Like Steve, many fathers today _____₂₂ (change) their ideas. They _____₂₃ (get) involved in the care and education of their children. These trends _____₂₄ (suggest) that soon, more and more fathers _____₂₅ (take) an active role in raising a family.

■ **YOUR TURN** What will Steve and his family be like in ten years? Will Steve be working? What will the children be doing? Are they going to appreciate his attitudes toward fatherhood? Imagine what will happen to this family and write a short ending to the story.

P A R T   S I X

Language Activities

These speaking and writing activities are designed to help you practice the past, present, and future verb tenses covered in this chapter.

SIMPLE PRESENT AND PRESENT CONTINUOUS TENSES

■ **ACTIVITY A** In pairs or in small groups, learn a little more about lifestyles in your classmates' cultures. Take turns describing some of the following.

1. a typical grandmother or grandfather in your culture
2. a typical teenager in your culture
3. a typical weekday for a typical family
4. a typical weekend
5. a typical holiday or special event such as a wedding
6. a typical house or apartment

As you share your ideas, be sure to include information or opinions about changes that are taking place in your culture.

■ **ACTIVITY B** Do you have any family pictures? In pairs or small groups, show pictures of your families. Describe the people in the pictures. Who are they, and where are they? What is each one doing?

SIMPLE PAST AND PAST CONTINUOUS TENSES

■ **ACTIVITY C** "The Family Circus" is a daily cartoon in the United States. Bill is the oldest child in the family. He has a bad habit of going places *indirectly*. Follow his path, telling step by step where he went and what he did.

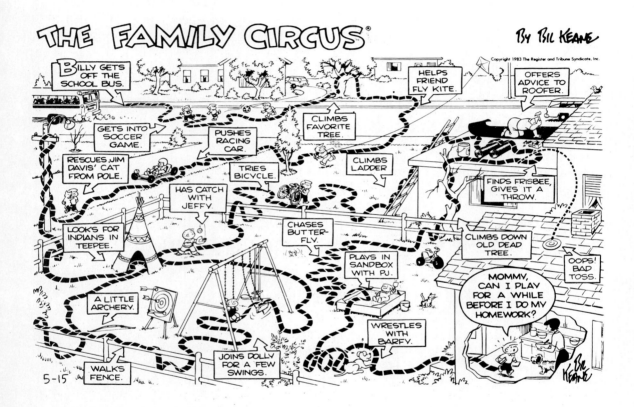

■ **ACTIVITY D** Your childhood may have been different from those of your classmates. Think of a few memorable events from your childhood and share them with the others. Separate into small groups and take turns telling stories. To get started, try to think of some of the funniest or most frightening, interesting, or awkward things that happened to you or your family. After you have finished, choose one story to use as the basis for a short composition.

SIMPLE FUTURE TENSE

■ **ACTIVITY E** In pairs or small groups, role-play the following scenes.

1. Imagine you are talking to your boyfriend or girlfriend.
    a. Make him or her an offer.
    b. Make him or her a promise.
    c. Make a prediction.
2. Imagine you are talking to your father or mother.
    a. Make him or her a promise.
    b. Make him or her a request.
3. Imagine you are talking to your teenage son or daughter.
    a. Make him or her a request.
    b. Make a prediction.

PRESENT PERFECT CONTINUOUS AND PRESENT PERFECT TENSES

■ **ACTIVITY F** Consider the current trends in your culture concerning changes in the family and in the roles of men and women. When did these changes begin? How have they developed? Have changes taking place in the United States affected your country?

In pairs or in small groups, compare some of the changes that have been taking place in your societies. Then choose one member of your group to give a brief summary of your discussion to the entire class.

CONTRAST OF TENSES

■ **ACTIVITY G** Every culture has favorite folk stories. Many of these often teach us lessons about life. Can you remember a folk story that you particularly liked as a child? In small groups, share some stories from your cultures. Do you find similar stories in different cultures? You may want to write these stories and make a short collection of folktales from around the world.

CHAPTER 2

Health

Modal Auxiliaries and Related Structures

In this chapter, you will study the forms and functions of the modal auxiliaries, as well as some structures related to them in usage. This chapter emphasizes the present forms, active voice. In Chapter 3, you will study the passive forms. In Chapter 8, you will study some of the past forms in more detail.

Previewing the Passage

What is good health to you? How do you maintain your health?

How Healthy Are You?

Good health is not something you are able to buy at a drugstore, and you can't depend on getting it back with a quick visit to a doctor when you're sick either. Making your body last without major problems has to be your own responsibil-ity. Mistreating your system by keeping bad habits, neglecting symptoms of
5   illness, and ignoring common health rules can counteract the best medical care.

Nowadays health specialists promote the idea of wellness for everybody. Wellness means achieving the best possible health within the limits of your body. One person may need many fewer calories than another. Some people might prefer a lot of easier exercise to more strenuous exercise. While one
10 person enjoys playing seventy-two holes of golf a week, another would rather play three sweaty, competitive games of tennis.

Understanding the needs of your own body is the key. Everyone runs the risk of accidents, and no one can be sure of avoiding chronic disease. Never-theless, poor diet, stress, a bad working environment, and carelessness or
15 abuse can ruin good health. By changing your habits or the conditions surrounding you, you can lower the risk or reduce the damage of disease.

Understanding Vocabulary

1. In the passage, what word means *health* and has the opposite mean-ing of *sickness* or *illness*? According to the passage, what does this word mean?
2. Find a word in the first paragraph that doctors use to mean *signs* or *indications*.
3. Which word does not belong?
   a. mistreat
   b. neglect
   c. ignore
   d. abuse
   e. take care of
4. Find two expressions in the passage that use *risk*. Explain them.

Discussing Ideas

1. In your opinion, what are some characteristics of a healthy person? Try to name at least five.
2. What is the general attitude toward health and health care in your culture?
3. How do general attitudes about health and health care in North America differ from those in your country or culture?

P A R T   O N E

Modals of Ability and Expectation

ARE YOU PHYSICALLY FIT?

- Physically fit people can go through a busy day and feel good the next morning.
- They are able to lift approximately one-half their body weight.
- They can bend and twist easily in all directions.
- They should be able to stay the same weight.

MODAL AUXILIARIES

A modal has only one form for all persons of the verb, but it can have several meanings and time frames, depending on the context. A complete list of modal auxiliaries and related structures appears on pages 260 and 261.

MODAL AUXILIARIES AND RELATED STRUCTURES EXPRESSING ABILITY

PRESENT ABILITY

can (cannot) **(not) be able to** } + simple form	John **can** run five miles, but I **can't** (cannot). How many miles **are** you **able to** run?	Affirmative and negative statements and questions all give the meaning of ability. In rapid speech, *can* is weakly stressed (kin). *Can't* is stressed more strongly.

PAST ABILITY

could (not) **(not) be able to** } + simple form	He **couldn't** run as fast as she **could.** I **wasn't able to** run because of the rain.	

■ **EXERCISE A** It is often difficult to distinguish between *can* and *can't* in rapid conversation. Of course, there is a tremendous difference in meaning! As your teacher rapidly reads the following sentences, circle *can* or *can't* according to what you hear.

1. I (can / can't) swim a mile.
2. John (can / can't) run a mile.
3. I (can / can't) walk a mile.
4. She (can / can't) ski very well.

5. He (can / can't) jog ten miles.
6. They (can / can't) skate very well.

■ **EXERCISE B** The chart that follows gives you the approximate calories you burn in sports and other activities. Use the information to form at least five sentences with *can*.

Example   You (A person) can burn over 300 calories by walking briskly for an hour.

CALORIES BURNED PER HOUR	ACTIVITY
72 – 84	sitting and talking
120 – 150	walking at a slow pace
240 – 300	doing housework (cleaning, mopping, scrubbing)
300 – 360	walking briskly, playing doubles tennis, playing Ping-Pong (table tennis)
350 – 420	bicycling, ice- or roller-skating
420 – 480	playing singles tennis
480 – 600	downhill skiing, jogging
600 – 650	running (5.5 mph), bicycling (13 mph)
over 660	running (6 or more mph), handball, squash, swimming (depends on stroke and style — an excellent overall conditioner)

Note: Food produces energy. One ounce of fat gives 267 calories of energy. A pound of fat is equivalent to 4,272 calories.

■ **YOUR TURN** Which of these sports do you know how to do? Which don't you know how to play? Give at least five original sentences using *can* (*not*), *could* (*not*), or (*not*) *be able to*.

Example   I can swim, but I'm not able to swim long distances anymore. When I was younger, I could.
or
I can ski, but I can't swim.

■ **EXERCISE C** The following list includes movements that physically fit people should be able to do. Using *can, could,* or *be able to,* work with a classmate to assess your own physical fitness. Compare how well you can do these activities with how well you were able to do them at age fifteen. Take turns asking each other questions; then decide together how physically fit you both are.

Examples   STUDENT A: **How fast can you walk or run?**
              STUDENT B: **Can you walk a mile in fifteen minutes?**

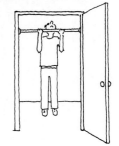

- walk or run a mile in less than fifteen minutes
- bicycle ten miles
- lift one-half your weight over your head
- do six push-ups in a row
- do three chin-ups in a row
- touch your toes without bending your legs
- kick your foot above shoulder height
- sit cross-legged without something to support your back

■ **YOUR TURN** Individually or in pairs, make a list of at least five things you can do now that you couldn't do ten years ago. Then make another list of at least five things you could do as a child that you can't do now. These may include the sports you play, the languages you speak, the type of clothing you wear, and so on.

MODAL AUXILIARIES OF EXPECTATION

PRESENT EXPECTATION

should (not) ⎫ **ought (not) to** ⎭ + simple form	The doctor **should** arrive at any minute. Your appointment **shouldn't** take long. **Shouldn't** she arrive soon? That medicine **ought to** be here today.	*Should* and *ought to* mean "will probably." *Should* is more common than *ought to.* Negative questions with *should* are often used for added emphasis. /Otta/ is the rapid pronunciation of *ought to.*

■ **EXERCISE D** Change the following sentences to use *should* or *ought to* instead of *expect*. You will need to change the subject in each sentence.

Example   We expect the doctor to arrive at any minute.
The doctor should arrive at any minute.
(The doctor ought to arrive at any minute.)

1. We expect the doctor to be here in a few minutes.
2. We don't expect the doctor to be very late.
3. The doctor expects the exam to take only a short time.
4. The doctor expects your exam to be normal.
5. She doesn't expect you to need another checkup for at least a year.
6. You can expect your bill to arrive within a week.

■ **EXERCISE E** **Review of Ability and Expectation** Complete the following, using *be able to, can, could,* or *should*. Use each form at least once.

Before

1. Before I began exercising at Ernie's Exercise Emporium,

    I _wasn't able to lose_ (not lose) weight, and I

    _____ (not find) any clothes that fit

    me well.

After

2. Now I _____ (lift) 300 pounds with

    one hand, but I _____ (not find / still)

    any clothes that fit me!

Before

3. Before I began exercising at Ernie's Exercise Emporium,

    I _____ (not run), I _____

    (not jog), I _____ (not walk), I

    _____ (not sit / even) without getting

    tired. I _____ (not do) anything!

After

4. Now I _____ (not do / still) anything!

    But the doctor says that I _____ (be)

    able to leave the hospital soon.

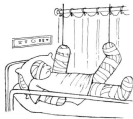

PART TWO

Modals of Request, Permission, and Preference

OFFICE VISITS

RECEPTIONIST: May I help you?
PATIENT: Could I see a dentist, fast?!

MODAL AUXILIARIES OF REQUEST AND PERMISSION

REQUEST FOR ACTION

Would you mind . . . ? + gerund (verb + *-ing*)	**Would** you **mind** calling a doctor? **Would** you **mind not** talking so loudly?	*Would you mind* is always followed by a gerund. A negative response means "I will." Informal answers are often affirmative, however.
Would you . . . ? **Could you . . . ?** **Can you . . . ?** **Will you . . . ?** + simple form	**Would** you call a doctor, please? **Could** you call Dr. Fox? **Can** you please come soon? **Will** you please come immediately?	*Please* is often added to any request. *Could* and *would* are appropriate in most circumstances. *Can* is informal, and it is used among friends. *Will* can be rude in tone. It is used in urgent situations or among friends.

⟶

REQUEST FOR PERMISSION

Would you mind if I . . . ? + past form	**Would** you mind if I came late for my appointment?	*Would you mind if I* is always followed by the past tense of a second verb. It is polite and formal. A negative response means "It's all right."
May I . . . ? ⎫ **Could I . . . ?** ⎬ **Can I . . . ?** ⎭ + simple form	**May** I help you?	*May* is formal. It is most often used in service situations.
	Could I talk with the doctor?	*May* and *could* are preferred in polite speech.
	Can I see the nurse?	*Can* is very informal, but it is often used in conversation.

Note: In rapid speech, *would, could,* and *can* are seldom pronounced clearly.

Would you . . . ? /wudja/   Would he . . . ? /wuddi/
Could you . . . ? /kudja/   Could he . . . ? /kuddi/
Can you . . . ? /kenya/   Can he . . . ? /keni/

■ **EXERCISE A** In an emergency, being polite is not as important as taking care of the situation. In emergencies, people often use commands. In most other circumstances, abrupt commands are considered rude.

Imagine that you are in a first aid class (not in an emergency situation). In pairs, take turns making and responding to requests. Change the following commands to polite requests for action by using *could, would,* or *would you mind.*

Example Quick! Call the doctor!
STUDENT A: **Would you please call the doctor?**
STUDENT B: **Certainly. Which doctor would you like me to call?**

1. Hurry! Get me some bandages!
2. Find some clean towels!
3. Open all the windows!
4. Don't touch that!
5. Help me move this!
6. Wash your hands!
7. Get a blanket!
8. Hold this!

■ **YOUR TURN**   Role-play the following requests.

1. You are in a movie theater. The person next to you is talking. Ask him or her to be quiet.
2. You are in an elevator, and someone is smoking. Ask the person not to smoke.
3. You are at home, and it is 1:30 A.M. Your neighbors are making a lot of noise. Ask them to be quiet.

■ **EXERCISE B**   In pairs, take turns making and responding to requests for permission. Complete the following conversations by using *may, could,* or *can*. Remember that *can* is informal and may not be appropriate for all situations.

Example   see the nurse
I'm sorry, but . . .
STUDENT A: **May (Could) I see the nurse?**
STUDENT B: **I'm sorry, but she's not available at the moment.**

1. make an appointment now
   Yes, of course . . .
2. speak with Dr. Fox
   I'm sorry, but . . .
3. get this prescription filled
   Certainly, . . .
4. pay by check
   Yes, if . . .

■ **YOUR TURN**   Role-play asking for the following.

1. You would like to borrow your sister's (brother's, roommate's) bicycle or car.
2. You need to use a telephone. Ask a stranger (your teacher, the school administrator) for change.
3. You would like to use your sister's (brother's, roommate's) favorite sweater (jacket, coat).

■ **EXERCISE C**   In pairs, complete the following conversations asking for permission or for action. Use *Can, Could, May, Would, Would you mind,* or *Would you mind if* in your requests. Use each form at least once.

Example   **Would you mind helping me for a little while?**
No, I wouldn't. I'd be happy to help you.

1. _____

Of course. When would you like to see the doctor?

2. _____

No problem! I can stop by the pharmacy for you.

3. _____

Sure, I could. Where do you want to go?

4. _____

Of course I wouldn't mind! What would you like me to do?

5. _____

No, not at all. Open as many windows as you like.

6. _____

Sure. I don't need that book for several days.

7. _____

No, I wouldn't. I'd be happy if you joined me.

8. _____

Thank you, but I'm just looking.

MODAL AUXILIARIES OF PREFERENCE

PRESENT PREFERENCES

I would rather (not) . . .
Would you rather (not) . . . ?
Wouldn't you rather . . . ?
+ simple form

I'd rather not come in the afternoon.
Would you **rather** come in the morning or the afternoon?
Wouldn't you **rather** come in the morning?

Affirmative and negative statements and questions with *would rather* express preferences or choices. The contracted form (*I'd, you'd*, etc.) is almost always used in conversational English.

I would (not) like . . .
Would you like . . . ?
Wouldn't you like . . . ?
+ infinitive or noun

I would like an appointment.
Would you **like** to see Dr. Jones?
I would like (prefer) to see Dr. Fox.
Wouldn't you **like (prefer)** to see the doctor sooner?

Affirmative and negative statements and questions with *would like* (*prefer*) may express desires or preferences. *Would like* (*prefer*) is followed by either a noun or an infinitive. It is often used in contracted form.

■ **EXERCISE D**   In pairs, take turns making suggestions and stating preferences with the following cues. Remember that *would like* is followed by an infinitive.

Example   go to a movie tonight / stay home
        STUDENT A: **Would (Wouldn't) you like to go to a movie tonight?**
        STUDENT B: **To be honest, I'd rather stay home.**

1. have Italian food for dinner / make Chinese food
2. go out for dinner / not spend money
3. visit New York this weekend / not go to a big city
4. take a long vacation / take several short trips
5. live at the ocean / live in the mountains
6. work for a major company / start my own business
7. live in Paris / spend time in Rome
8. see a play tonight / study English grammar

■ **YOUR TURN**   With a new partner, make your own suggestions and responses. They may include suggestions about movies, restaurants, trips, classes, concerts, and so on.

■ **EXERCISE E   Review of Requests, Permissions, and Preferences**   Add appropriate words or phrases to complete the following conversation.

RECEPTIONIST: Good afternoon. Doctor's office. *Would*_____ you
        *mind*_____ holding for a minute? (*click*) Hello.
        Thank you for holding. _____₁
        _____₂ help you?

ESTELA: Hello. This is Estela Ortiz. I _____₃

_____₄ to make an appointment to see Dr.

Fox soon for a checkup.

RECEPTIONIST: Dr. Fox will be on vacation for the next three weeks.

_____₅ _____₆ like _____₇

see one of the other doctors?

ESTELA: No, I'd _____₈ wait to see Dr. Fox. When is

the earliest that I _____₉ schedule an ap-

pointment?

RECEPTIONIST: He has openings during the week of September 12.

Would _____₁₀ _____₁₁ come in the

morning or in the afternoon?

ESTELA: I_____₁₂ _____₁₃ not come in the

morning. _____₁₄ _____₁₅ give me

an appointment after 4:00 P.M. on either Tuesday or

Thursday?

RECEPTIONIST: I _____₁₆ schedule you for 4:15, Tuesday

afternoon.

ESTELA: Thanks. That'll be fine.

PART THREE

Modals of Need and Advice

MEDICAL EMERGENCIES

Everyone ought to know the basic steps to follow in case of a medical emergency. If you don't, you should contact your local Red Cross. The Red Cross gives guidelines and offers short courses on what to do in emergency situations.

MODAL AUXILIARIES AND RELATED STRUCTURES EXPRESSING NEED AND LACK OF NEED

PRESENT NEED

must (not) ⎫ **have to** ⎬ + simple form	You **must** practice every day if you want to improve.	In affirmative statements and questions, *must* and *have to* have similar meanings. Both mean "need to."
	John **has to** study, so he can't play today.	In rapid speech, *have to* and *has to* sound like /hafta/ and /hasta/.
	You **must not** let tennis interfere with your work.	*Must not* expresses a strong need *not* to do something.

PRESENT LACK OF NEED

don't (doesn't) have to + simple form	I **don't have to** study, so I can play tennis.	In negative statements, *do/does not have to* refers to something that it is *not* necessary to do. Its meaning is very different from *must not*.

PAST NEED

had to + simple form	I **had to** make reservations for a tennis court. **Did** you **have to** give them a deposit?	In affirmative statements and questions, *had to* implies that the action was completed.

PAST LACK OF NEED

didn't have to + simple form	I **didn't have to** give a deposit. We **didn't have to** pay in advance.	In negative statements, *did not have to* refers to something that it was *not* necessary to do.

■ **EXERCISE A** Change commands using *must/must not.*

Example Don't use electrical appliances in the water!
You must not use electrical appliances in the water!

1. Call a doctor right away!
2. Get an ambulance immediately!
3. Don't move!
4. Don't touch that!
5. Turn off the electricity!
6. Find someone to help!

■ **EXERCISE B** Read the following guidelines for emergencies. Then complete the sentences with *must not* or *don't/doesn't have to.*

The American Red Cross gives these guidelines to follow in emergency situations.

1. If necessary, rescue the victim as quickly and carefully as possible.
2. Call for medical help immediately.
3. Check to see if the victim is breathing and give him or her artificial respiration if necessary.
4. Control severe bleeding.
5. If you suspect poisoning, immediately give a conscious victim water or milk to dilute* the poison. If the victim is unconscious or having convulsions,† however, do not give any fluids.
6. In an accident, do **not** move the victim unless absolutely necessary.
7. Always check for injuries **before** moving the victim if possible.

Example If the victim has a neck injury, you _**must not**_____ move him or her.

1. If you _____ make an emergency rescue, do not move the victim.

2. You _____ move a person with a neck or back injury unless absolutely necessary.

3. If your victim has swallowed a poison and is unconscious, you _____ give him or her anything.

4. You _____ study first aid, but it may be helpful someday.

5. A person who knows first aid _____ call a doctor about every small accident.

---
* *dilute* make thinner or weaker
† *convulsions* violent muscle contractions

■ **EXERCISE C** Read the following medicine label. Then rephrase the instructions to tell what the user *must* or *must not* do. Make at least five statements.

Example   **You must not use this medicine if the printed seal is not intact.**

USE ONLY IF PRINTED SEAL UNDER CAP IS INTACT.

Adult Dose: Use only as directed by your physician.

WARNINGS: Do not give this medicine to children under age 12. Keep this and all drugs out of the reach of children. In case of an overdose, contact a physician or a poison control center immediately. Do not use this product if you are pregnant or nursing a baby. Do not use this product while operating a vehicle or machinery. Consult your physician before using this product if you have any of the following conditions: heart problems, high blood pressure, asthma.

■ **EXERCISE D Past Needs with *Had to*.**   Imagine that you took a class in first aid and practiced an emergency situation, a fire in an apartment. Tell what you *had to do* by changing these commands to past tense statements with *had to*.

Example   Rescue the victims quickly and carefully!
            We had to rescue the victims.

1. Call the fire department fast!
2. Get a doctor!
3. Check the victims carefully!
4. Give the child artificial respiration immediately!
5. Check the man for injuries!
6. Control the bleeding from the man's wounds!

■ **YOUR TURN**   Have you been in an emergency situation? What did you have to do?

MODAL AUXILIARIES AND RELATED STRUCTURES EXPRESSING ADVICE

PRESENT ADVICE

had better (not) **should (not)** **ought (not) to** + simple form	He **had better** lose some weight. He **had better not** gain more weight. You **should** get more exercise. **Should** I start on an exercise program? You **ought to** start tomorrow.	*Had better, should,* and *ought to* all express advice. *Had better* and *ought to* are seldom used in questions, however. In rapid speech, *you'd better* often sounds like /ya bedder/, and *ought to* sounds like /otta/.

PAST ADVICE (NOT TAKEN)

should (not) have **ought (not) to have** + past participle	You **should have** spent more time practicing. **Should** I **have** practiced every day? We **ought to have** played much better than we did.	*Should have* and *ought to have* give advice about past actions or situations. *Ought to have* is seldom used in questions, however. Both imply that the subject did not complete the action or take the advice. In rapid speech, these sound like /shudda/ and /ottuv/.

■ **EXERCISE E** In pairs, take turns making the following statements and responding to them. Make suggestions from the phrases in parentheses or invent your own suggestions. Use *had better, ought to,* and *should.*

Example STUDENT A: My knee has been swollen and sore since I played tennis. (go to a doctor)
STUDENT B: **You'd better go to a doctor.**

1. I've had a headache for several hours. (take a break from studying)
2. I've had a toothache since last week. (see a dentist)
3. I can't see well at night anymore. (have your eyes checked)
4. I can't get rid of this cold. (stay in bed for a few days)
5. None of my clothes fit anymore. (go on a diet)

■ **EXERCISE F** Change the following from commands to statements by using *should* or *should not*.

Example   If someone feels faint

- Have the person lie flat with his head low.
- Make the person lower his head between his knees and breathe deeply.

If someone feels faint, you should have him lie flat and keep his head low. You should make him breathe deeply.

1. If someone cuts herself seriously
    - Try to stop the bleeding at once.
    - Use a clean bandage to cover the wound.
    - Do not remove the bandage when the bleeding stops.
    - Try to raise the wound up high.

2. If you suspect a broken bone
    - Don't let the victim bend the surrounding joints (knee, ankle, elbow, etc.).
    - Give first aid for shock.
    - Don't touch an open wound.
    - Cover the wound gently.

3. If you suspect a head injury
    - Keep the person quiet.
    - If possible, do not move her.
    - Loosen the clothing around her neck.
    - Do not give her any stimulants (coffee, tea, etc.).

4. If someone burns himself (first- or second-degree burns)
    - Apply lukewarm water until the pain goes away.
    - Dry the burned area very gently.
    - Cover the burn with a bandage to protect it if necessary.
    - Do not break any blisters or remove any skin.

■ **EXERCISE G** In rapid conversation, it is often difficult to distinguish present and perfect modals. As your teacher reads the following sentences, circle the modal forms (present or perfect) that you hear.

1. They (should come / should have come).
2. He (ought to set / ought to have set) a specific time.
3. She (should become / should have become) a doctor.
4. She (ought to quit / ought to have quit) her job.
5. It (should cost / should have cost) less.
6. We (shouldn't let / shouldn't have let) that happen.

■ **EXERCISE H** In pairs, respond to the following sentences with a statement using either *should have* or *ought to have*.

Example   Jack studied first aid last semester.
          I should have studied it too, but I didn't.

1. Veronica went to the dentist last week.
2. Centa ran six miles this morning.
3. Midori took an exercise class last quarter.
4. Ted swam for two hours this morning.
5. Futoshi had a checkup yesterday.
6. Nancy rode her bicycle to school today.

■ **EXERCISE I** Veronica was the first to arrive at a car accident. She tried to help, but she panicked and did everything wrong. Use the information from Exercise F to help you tell what she *should (not)/ought (not) to have done.*

Example   A young girl had a burn from an accident. Veronica washed the burn with hot water.
          Veronica shouldn't have washed the burn with hot water. She should have applied lukewarm water until the pain stopped.

1. One man fainted. Veronica made him stand up quickly.
2. A woman had a head injury. Veronica had the woman walk around and drink several cups of coffee.
3. A boy had serious cuts. Veronica let the boy bleed for a few minutes. Then she covered the wound with a newspaper.
4. Another man had a broken arm. Veronica moved his elbow and shoulder to check them.

PART FOUR

Modals of Possibility and Probability

Answer: 4. All of the above.

TEST YOUR KNOWLEDGE OF SYMPTOMS

You are at the scene of an accident. The victim is weak, pale, and dizzy. His pulse is fast, the pupils of his eyes are different sizes, and his arm is swollen and painful.

1. The victim may be in shock.
2. The victim might have a head injury.
3. The victim may have broken his arm.
4. All of the above.

MODAL AUXILIARIES EXPRESSING POSSIBILITY AND PROBABILITY

PRESENT POSSIBILITY

may (not) **might (not)** **could (not)** + simple form	He **may** have a bad case of the flu. He **might** have a bad cold. He **might not** come to school tomorrow. **Could** he have pneumonia?	In affirmative and negative statements, *may (have)*, *might (have)*, and *could (have)* all express possibility. All mean "possibly" or "perhaps."

PAST POSSIBILITY

may (not) have **might (not) have** **could (not) have** + past participle	She **may have** hurt her leg. She **might have** broken her leg. She **couldn't have** broken it.	*May* is not used with questions with this meaning. In rapid speech, *may have* is pronounced /mayuv/ *might have* is pronounced /mightuv/, and *could have* is pronounced /coulduv/.

PRESENT PROBABILITY

must (not) + simple form	You **must** be in shock from the accident. Your head **must** hurt a lot! You **must not** feel good.	*Must* and *must have* express probability. Both mean "probably." *Must* is not used in questions with this meaning. In rapid speech, *must have* is pronounced /mustuv/.

PAST PROBABILITY

must (not) have + past participle	You **must have** been in shock right after the accident. Your head **must have** hurt very much. You **must not have** felt good.	*Must have* expresses probability in the past. It does not express need.

■ **EXERCISE A** In medicine, the clues used in making "educated guesses" are called *symptoms*. Use the information in the following chart or your own knowledge to diagnose the symptoms below. Use *may, might,* or *could* to make your diagnoses.

SYMPTOMS	POSSIBLE INJURY OR ILLNESS
If the victim is weak, pale, thirsty, cool, nauseated, or sweaty— If the pulse is fast but weak—	the person may be in shock.
If the victim is dizzy or bleeding from the nose, ears, or mouth— If the pulse is slow and strong *or* fast and weak— If the victim cannot move an arm or leg— If the pupils* of the eyes are different sizes—	the person may have a head injury.
If the victim's knee, wrist, ankle, (etc.) is swollen, tender, bruised, or painful when moved—	the person may have sprained a joint (knee, wrist, ankle, etc.).
If the victim's arm, leg, hip, (etc.) is swollen, tender to the touch, bruised, very painful when moved, or deformed in shape—	the person may have broken a bone (arm, leg, hip, etc.).
If the victim is coughing, nauseated, or dizzy— If the victim has pain in the chest, trouble breathing, or a bluish color in the lips and around the fingernails—	the person may have had a heart attack.

Example   The victim is weak and pale.
             The victim could be in shock.

1. The victim's pulse is fast.
2. The victim is dizzy.
3. The victim's knee is swollen.
4. The victim is very thirsty.
5. The victim's pupils are different sizes.
6. The victim feels great pain when his arm is moved.

* *pupil* center point in the eye

■ **EXERCISE B**   Use *may, might,* or *could have* to make additional diagnoses.

Example   The victim was playing soccer. His knee is very tender. It is swollen.
He may have sprained his knee.

1. The victim suddenly felt sharp pains in his chest. He is breathing with great difficulty.
2. The victim fell while roller-skating. Her wrist is swollen and tender. She cannot move it without a great deal of pain.
3. The victim was in a car accident. She is dizzy, and she cannot move her arm.
4. The victim was jogging. His ankle and the back of his leg are very sore.

■ **EXERCISE C**   In pairs, take turns making statements and responses. Use *must* with the cues in parentheses to form your responses.

Example   I didn't sleep very well last night. (be tired)
You must be tired.

1. The food at lunch today was very salty. (be thirsty)
2. The food at the cafeteria is good today. (have a new cook)
3. Every time I work in the garden, I sneeze a lot. (be allergic to something)
4. I burned my hand on the stove last night. (hurt)
5. I can't read signs when I'm driving. (need glasses)
6. My friend sprained her knee playing tennis. (not be able to walk very well)

■ **YOUR TURN**   Is anyone absent from your class today? Does anyone look particularly excited or happy? Does anyone look worried? Try to guess why.

Example   George's not here.
He may be sick.
He might have gone away for a long weekend.
He must not have done his homework!

■ **EXERCISE D**   In pairs, use the cues and take turns making statements and responses with *must have.*

Example   break / leg
walk
STUDENT A: **I broke my leg last year.**
STUDENT B: **It must have been difficult for you to walk.**

1. break / jaw
   eat
2. sprain / wrist
   write
3. have / ear infection
   hear
4. drink / coffee constantly
   sleep
5. have / noisy roommates
   study

■ **EXERCISE E Review of Modals**   Make statements about each of the following.

Example   The Nelsons are coming here for dinner around 6:00. It's 5:00.
Expectation: **They should arrive in about an hour.**

1. I haven't put the roast in the oven yet.

   Advice: _____

2. The house is a mess.

   Advice: _____

   Past advice: _____

3. I don't have enough time to get everything ready by 6:00.

   Past advice: _____

   Possibility: _____

4. I'm going to call the Nelsons to ask them to come at 6:30.

   Request (to the Nelsons): _____

5. It's 6:45, and the Nelsons are not here yet.

   Possibility: _____

   Possibility: _____

6. It's 6:50, and the phone is ringing.

   Probability: _____

7. The Nelsons are at the hospital.

   Present or past probability: _____

   Request (to the Nelsons): _____

8. Twins were born — Martin and Marina!

   Present probability: _____

P A R T   F I V E

Language Activities

These speaking and writing activities are designed to help you practice the modal auxiliaries and related structures covered in this chapter.

MODAL AUXILIARIES OF ABILITY AND EXPECTATION

■ **ACTIVITY A** In recent years, Americans have become very concerned about their health. In fact, physical fitness has become almost a national obsession. In large cities and small towns alike, people jog regularly, join sports teams, and go to health clubs to work out. What is the attitude toward health and physical fitness in your culture? Is fitness important? Are there differences in fitness for males and females? In small groups, prepare a brief report on the attitudes toward health and fitness in your cultures. Describe a typical "physically fit" man and woman in each culture and note any similarities or differences in cultural attitudes.

MODAL AUXILIARIES OF REQUEST AND PERMISSION

■ **ACTIVITY B** Have you been to the doctor or dentist recently? Will you see one soon? In pairs, practice making telephone calls to arrange appointments. Role-play making appointments by phone for the following statements.

1. a routine medical checkup
2. getting your teeth cleaned
3. an emergency such as a severe pain in your side

MODAL AUXILIARIES OF PREFERENCE

Imagine that you have won a two-week vacation at the health spa of your choice, all expenses paid! You will be able to spend two weeks getting in shape! Where would you like to go? Would you go to a mountain health resort and spend your time hiking and climbing? Would you go to the ocean and swim? Or would you rather go to a desert area and play golf?

In pairs or small groups, discuss your "trips" and then tell the class about your plans. Remember that you must plan some physical activity.

PRESENT NEEDS WITH *HAVE TO* AND PRESENT PREFERENCES

What do you have to do this week? What would you rather do? In pairs or small groups, discuss your "To Do's" and "Would Rather's." Then write out your lists.

PAST NEEDS WITH *HAD TO*

What did you have to do to come to this city or this area? What did you have to do to begin studying at this school? List at least eight things that you had to do in order to be here now.

MODAL AUXILIARIES AND RELATED STRUCTURES EXPRESSING NEED AND ADVICE

■ **ACTIVITY C** In pairs or in small groups, give advice on the following topics or choose some topics of particular interest to you. Be sure to use a variety of modals of advice and need as you discuss your topics.

1. how to get in shape
2. how to enjoy the beach without getting too much sun
3. how to develop a good tennis serve
4. how to quit smoking

CHAPTER 3

Technology

The Passive Voice

In this chapter, you will study the forms and uses of verbs in the passive voice. The time frame of a passive verb is generally the same as the time frame of an active verb, but the focus of the passive sentence is different. As you study the chapter, pay careful attention to the focus of passive constructions.

Previewing the Passage

Tele, from Greek, means "far" or "far off." It appears in words like *telegraph, telephone,* and *telecommunications.* Telecommunications— communications from far away—are a normal part of our world today, but has this been true for very long?

Developments in Telecommunications

During most of human history, communication was limited by time and distance. In less than 200 years, however, revolutionary changes in communication have occurred. In the nineteenth century, the telegraph and telephone were invented. Radio, television, and computers were developed in the twentieth
5   century. These inventions completely changed people's lives around the world.

Today all of these communications devices are being linked together, creating a worldwide "information" revolution. This new wave of technology is called "telecommunications"—the use of electronic media (television, radio, telephones, and computers) to communicate across distance and time. Tele-
10   phones are now connected to home computers and television sets, radio stations are linked to home computers, and home computers are tied to news publishing services.

Much of this is possible because of new technology that is known as fiber optics—communication lines that are made of glass fibers. Because of glass-
16   fiber technology, large amounts of information may be sent at great speed over telephone and cable television lines.

Today the world can be linked instantly by computers and satellites. All of our systems—economic, social, and political—are already being affected by these tools of technology. In the not-too-distant future, *everyone* will be af-
20   fected by these and further developments in telecommunications.

Understanding Vocabulary

1. Technology is scientific or technical knowledge that we use for a practical purpose. In the twentieth century, we have seen incredible advances in technology. From your own experience, try to list at least three examples of older technology and newer technology.

OLDER TECHNOLOGY

Example   dial phones

a. _____

b. _____

c. _____

NEWER TECHNOLOGY

Example   cellular phones

a. _____

b. _____

c. _____

2. Match the words with similar meanings.

worldwide	device
develop	link
connect	global
tool	invent

3. Complete the sentences with forms of the word *develop*.

   a. Today scientists are _____ many new devices

   in the telecommunications industry.

   b. Scientists have already _____ new glass-fiber

   technology.

   c. Soon everyone will be affected in some way by these new

   _____ .

Discussing Ideas

1. Imagine communications 300 years ago. How did people in different towns, cities, and countries communicate with one another?
   Think about communications 60 years ago. How did your relatives
   communicate with one another?
2. What new communications devices has the world seen during the
   last 100 years? What devices have you seen in your lifetime?
3. How is your world changing because of all the new technology in
   telecommunications?

PART ONE

Passive Voice—Simple Tenses

THE IMPACT OF INVENTIONS

During most of human history, even the most
important news was difficult to deliver.
Then, in the 1800s, the telegraph and telephone were invented. Today these inventions are taken for granted, and people are
frustrated if a telephone call does not go
through!

INTRODUCTION TO PASSIVE VOICE

Most transitive verbs (verbs that take an object) can be used in the passive voice as well as in the active voice. In sentences in the active voice, primary focus is on the subject (the agent or doer of the action). To change the focus of the sentence, use the passive voice. The passive voice occurs in both spoken and written English, and it is used frequently in technical writing.

FORMATION OF PASSIVE VOICE

The object in the active voice becomes the subject in the corresponding sentence in the passive voice. The agent (the active-voice subject) is sometimes included in passive sentences to tell who or what did the action. A form of the verb *be* is always used in passive sentences. It is singular or plural to agree with the subject; it also tells the tense of the passive construction.

	subject *verb* *direct object*
Active	Alexander Graham Bell **invented** the telephone.
Passive	The telephone **was invented** by Alexander Graham Bell. *agent*

	subject *verb* *direct object*
Active	Millions of people **use** telephones every day.
Passive	Telephones **are used** by millions of people every day. *agent*

In active-voice sentences with both a direct and an indirect object, either object may become the subject of the corresponding passive sentence. This occurs more frequently with the indirect object than with the direct object, however.

	subject *verb* *indirect object* *direct object*
Active	The United States **gave** Bell the patent for the telephone.
Passive	The patent for the telephone **was given** to Bell by the United States.
	Bell **was given** the patent for the telephone by the United States.

$\longrightarrow$

PASSIVE VOICE—SIMPLE TENSES

The passive voice of verbs in simple tenses is formed in this way: *be* (*am, is, are, was, were*) + past participle (+ *by* + agent). Adverbs of frequency usually come after the auxiliary *be*. The passive forms have the same general meanings and time frames as verbs in the active voice. The focus of the passive sentence shifts, however.

	ACTIVE	PASSIVE
Simple past	Samuel Morse **invented** the Morse code.	The Morse code **was invented** by Samuel Morse.
Focus:	Samuel Morse	the Morse code
Simple present	Telegraph operators still **use** the Morse code today.	The Morse code **is** still **used** by telegraph operators today.
Focus:	telegraph operators	the Morse code

■ **EXERCISE A**   Complete the following by using either the present or past tense of the verbs in parentheses. Use the passive voice.

Example   Until 1845 and the invention of the telegraph, most communication *was carried* (carry) from place to place by messengers.

1. Before the telegraph, the speed of communication _____ _____ (limit) by the speed of transportation.

2. History _____ (fill) with examples of efforts to communicate news quickly, such as Pheidippides' 26-mile, 385-yard (42.2-km) run to bring the news of the Greek victory at Marathon.

1876

3. Until 1876, most day-to-day information _____ (communicate) by letters, newspapers, or conversation.

4. The telephone _____ (invent) in 1876.

5. Today the telephone _____ (take) for granted by much of the world.

1886

1927

1990

6. According to Marshall McLuhan, "The telephone began as a novelty, became a necessity, and _____ (regard / now) as an absolute right."

7. Over 400 million telephones _____ (use) daily by people throughout the world.

8. Between 1950 and 1975, over 2.3 trillion (2,300,000,000,000) telephone calls _____ (made) by Bell Telephone customers in the United States.

■ **EXERCISE B**   First underline the phrase with *by* in each sentence. Then change the sentences from the passive voice to the active voice.

Example   In 1816, a simple telegraph was invented <u>by an Englishman, Francis Ronalds.</u>
An Englishman, Francis Ronalds, invented a simple telegraph in 1816.

1. The first practical telegraph was built by Harrison Gray Dyer in 1826.
2. Messages were sent by Dyer across eight miles of wire.
3. Later an alphabet code was developed by an American, Joseph Henry.
4. Until 1837, different codes were used by each inventor.
5. Then a standard code was introduced by Samuel Morse.
6. Morse code was soon adopted by all telegraph operators.

■ **EXERCISE C**   First underline the object(s) in each sentence. Then change the sentences from the active voice to the passive voice.

Example   A German, Philipp Reis, designed <u>an early telephone</u> in about 1861.
An early telephone was designed by Philipp Reis, a German, in about 1861.

1. In 1876, two inventors filed patent applications on the same day.
2. In 1876, Alexander Graham Bell, a Scot living in the United States, requested a patent for an electric telephone.
3. An American, Elisha Gray, applied for* a similar patent on the very same day.
4. Both Bell and Gray, working independently, developed similar telephones.
5. The U.S. Patent Office received Bell's application first.
6. The U.S. Patent Office gave the patent to Alexander Graham Bell.

---

* *Apply for* is an inseparable phrasal verb. The two words act as a unit in both the active and passive voices.

By + Agent

By + noun (or pronoun) can be used in passive sentences to tell who or what performed the action of the verb. However, most passive sentences in English do *not* contain these phrases. Use *by* + agent only if the phrase gives the following information.

Information important to the meaning of the sentence **A name or idea that is important in the context**	The majority of overseas phone calls are transmitted **by satellite.** The telephone was invented **by Alexander Graham Bell.** Telephones are made ~~by people~~ in factories.	*By* + agent must be used if the sentence is meaningless without it. Proper names are often included because they give specific information. Other nouns and pronouns are often omitted.
New or unusual information	Today most overseas calls are transmitted **by satellite.** The calls are beamed ~~by satellite~~ from one country to another.	*By* + agent is generally included if the phrase introduces new or unusual information. After the agent is understood, the phrase is usually omitted to avoid repetition.

■ **EXERCISE D**   The following sentences give you information about early telephones. First read all the sentences and underline the phrase with *by* in each sentence. Then decide whether each *by* + agent is necessary to the meaning of the sentence. Tell which phrases you would omit and explain why.

Examples   In the 1870s, a simple telephone was invented <u>by Alexander Graham Bell and Thomas Watson.</u>
Do not omit the phrase because it tells *who* invented the telephone.

The official U.S. patent for this telephone was issued <u>by the U.S. Patent Office</u> on March 7, 1876.
The phrase can be omitted. It is obvious from the passive subject that the patent was from the U.S. government.

1. In the same year, similar patents were applied for by other inventors.
2. Nevertheless, the patent was given to Bell by the U.S. Patent Office.

3. In Bell and Watson's first telephone, the human voice was changed to electricity by moving magnets.*
4. However, many problems were encountered by Bell and Watson with this system.
5. Finally, a new system of voice vibrations† was developed by Bell and Watson.
6. The basic idea of Bell and Watson's system is still used by companies in telephones today.

■ **YOUR TURN** Think of other developments in science, technology, business, education, or the arts. What was believed about these? How were they going to affect people's lives?

■ **EXERCISE E** Complete the following passage with either active or passive forms (simple present or past tenses) of the verbs in parentheses.

THE IMPACT OF THE TELEPHONE

Many new inventions _are used_____ (use) every day, but the telephone _became_____ (become) an everyday item faster than almost any other invention in history. In May 1877, six telephones _____₁ (be) in commercial use. In November 1877, there _____₂ (be) 3,000, and by the beginning of the 1800's, 133,000.

---

* *magnet* a body, such as a piece of metal, which attracts another substance
† *vibrations* quick, repeated movements back and forth or up and down

Today people everywhere _____₃ (affect) by the telephone, though most of us _____₄ (use) it without really thinking about it. In the beginning, however, many people _____₅ (fear) the telephone. It _____₆ (believe) by some that the telephone _____₇ (be) evil, and laws _____₈ (suggest) by a few to prohibit telephones in bedrooms in order to prevent secret conversations. (Telephones would allow private romantic conversations, and this would corrupt people, especially young girls!) But these ideas and fears _____₉ (forget) as the demand for telephones grew.

At first in the United States, young boys _____₁₀ (employ) by telephone companies, but because of their bad language and tricks, many of them _____₁₁ (lose) their jobs. In September 1878, Emma M. Nutt, whose photo appears above at the left _____₁₂ (hire) as the first woman telephone operator. In France, women _____₁₃ (employ) from the beginning. This was in part because all boys and young men _____14 (require) to serve in the army. More important, the female voice _____15 (sound) much clearer over early telephone lines.

In the late 1800s, the telephone, together with the typewriter, _____16 (bring) thousands of women to work in offices. New fashions _____17 (create) to suit the needs of female workers, and "appropriate" clothes for work _____18 (introduce / soon). The shirtwaist dress and the blouse _____19 (design) for women "going to business." The telephone, obviously, _____20 (help) begin the social revolution that _____21 (continue) today.

Today the telephone _____22 (be) a major part of our lives, and we _____23 (not notice / usually) it unless it _____24 (be) out of order. In fact, with over 300 million telephones worldwide, no other invention _____25 (use) so much.

PART TWO

Passive Voice — Perfect Tenses

GADGETS, GADGETS, AND MORE GADGETS!

In the last fifty years, our way of life has been revolutionized by gadgets of all types: television sets and VCRs, microwave ovens and garage-door openers, to name a few. Until the 1940s or the 1950s, however, many of these common household items had never been dreamed possible.

PASSIVE VOICE — PERFECT TENSES

The passive voice of verbs in perfect tenses is formed in this way: *have* (*has, have, had*) + *been* + past participle (+ *by* + agent). Adverbs of frequency usually come after the auxiliary *have*.

	ACTIVE	PASSIVE
Present perfect	New technology **has revolutionized** the communications industry.	The communications industry **has been revolutionized** by new technology.
Focus:	new technology	the communications industry
Past perfect	Before the 1950s, researchers **had not yet developed** high-quality audio and video equipment.	Before the 1950s, high-quality audio and video equipment **had not yet been developed.**
Focus:	researchers	high-quality audio and video equipment

■ **EXERCISE A** First underline the object in each sentence. Then change the sentences from the active to the passive voice. Omit the agent unless it is important to the meaning of the sentence.

Example   In just forty years, companies have introduced <u>an amazing selection of audio and video equipment</u>: color television, transistor radios, cassette players, video recorders, and compact discs.
In just forty years, an amazing selection of audio and video equipment has been introduced: color television, transistor radios, cassette players, video recorders, and compact discs.

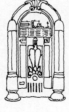   

1. In the past forty years, researchers have revolutionized audio and video technology.
2. By the mid-1950s, Ampex Corporation had introduced the first modern video recorder.
3. The television industry has used the Ampex system since that time.

4. By the late 1950s, companies had introduced the first stereo record.
5. Since 1960, researchers have developed high quality sound systems.
6. By the late 1980s, scientists had developed compact discs and light-weight camcorders.*
7. In recent years, MCA, RCA, and several European companies have designed and produced videodisc systems.

■ **EXERCISE B** Imagine you work in a recording studio, and you are going to videotape a TV commercial. In pairs, go over your final checklist before you begin recording. Ask questions using the present perfect tense of the passive voice. Give short answers using the past participle.

Example   call the actors
            STUDENT A: **Have the actors been called?**
            STUDENT B: **Called!**

1. test the microphones
2. check the lights
3. clean the camera lenses
4. focus the camera
5. test the loudspeakers
6. adjust the sound
7. load the film
8. close the doors

■ **EXERCISE C** Use simple present or present perfect forms of the verbs in parentheses. Choose between active and passive forms.

THOSE AMAZING MACHINES! (ALSO KNOWN AS MICROELECTRONIC DEVICES†)

In recent years, we _have grown_____ (grow) very dependent on machines of all kinds — in business, in industry, and in our own homes. In fact, the average person _____₁ (surround) by hundreds of devices that _____₂ (use) microelectronic technology. For example, this technology _____₃ (employ) in microwave ovens and digital clocks.

In only a few short years, microelectronic technology _____₄ (make) it possible to produce practical devices for everyday life. High-speed cameras with automatic focusing _____₅ (create). Compact-disc players _____₆ (develop).

---

* *camcorders* video camera–recorder combinations
† Microelectronics deals with electric currents in small components such as transistors and microchips. Microelectronic devices are found everywhere today.

Remote-control devices _____7 (produce) for televisions and video recorders, among other items.

Hundreds of microelectronic devices _____8 (exist) today, but all _____9 (construct) with similar types of components. These present-day solid-state components _____10 (be) smaller, cheaper, and more reliable than components of the past.

■ **YOUR TURN** Think about other microelectronic devices in your home, your workplace, and your school. Can you name a few that have been developed in recent years?

PART THREE

Passive Voice — Continuous Tenses

COMPUTERS AND YOU

It was only about fifty years ago that the first computer, Mark I, was being developed. Since then computers have affected every aspect of our lives. Today our phone calls are being directed by computers, our mail is being sorted by computers, and our children are being taught by computers.

PASSIVE VOICE — CONTINUOUS TENSES

The passive voice of verbs in continuous tenses is formed in this way: *be* (*am, is, are, was, were*) + *being* + past participle (+ *by* + agent). Adverbs of frequency generally come after the first auxiliary verb.

	ACTIVE	PASSIVE
Present continuous	Many companies **are using** computers for interoffice communication.	Computers **are being used** for interoffice communication.
Focus:	many companies	computers
Past continuous	Ten years ago, companies **were using** typewriters for most memos.	Ten years ago, typewriters **were being used** for most memos.
Focus:	companies	typewriters

■ **EXERCISE A** Change the following sentences to the passive voice. Omit *by* + agent if it is not necessary to the meaning of the sentence.

Example By 1944, people were operating the first computer.
By 1944, the first computer was being operated.

1. Soon people were using large computers in government and business.
2. During the 1950s, people were building computers with vacuum tubes.
3. By 1959, transistors were replacing the vacuum tubes.
4. By the 1960s, people were using electronic circuits in all computers.
5. By the early 1970s, people were developing the silicon chip.
6. Soon people were designing affordable microcomputers.
7. By the mid-1970s, stores everywhere were selling computers.
8. By the late 1980s, companies were producing laptop computers.

■ **EXERCISE B** Change the following sentences from the active voice to the passive voice. Omit the agent in later sentences to avoid repetition.

Example Computers are affecting people's jobs.
People's jobs are being affected by computers.

1. For example, computers are replacing workers on assembly lines.
2. Computers are also replacing office workers.
3. However, computers are creating new jobs in many fields.
4. Computers are training new employees through special programs.
5. Computers are running factory assembly lines.
6. Computers are teaching and testing students.

■ **EXERCISE C** Change the following sentences from the present continuous, active voice to the past continuous, passive voice.

Example   Today computers are typing letters. (secretaries)
Twenty years ago, letters were being typed by secretaries.

1. Today computers are addressing envelopes. (secretaries)
2. Computers are filling prescriptions. (pharmacists)
3. Today computers are sorting mail. (postal workers)
4. Computers are calculating bank balances. (accountants)
5. Computers are diagnosing illnesses. (doctors)
6. Today computers are figuring taxes. (accountants)

■ **EXERCISE D** Test your memory of information that was covered earlier in this chapter. In pairs, take turns asking and answering the following questions.

1. Was the telegraph being used in 1850?
2. Was Morse code being used with the telegraph in 1850?
3. Were telephones being used in 1860?
4. Were stereo records being used in the 1940s?
5. Were computers being used in the 1930s?
6. Were transistors being used in computers in 1955?
7. Was the silicon chip being used in computers in 1980?
8. Were compact discs being used in 1990?

■ **EXERCISE E Contrast of Tenses** Complete the following passage with either the active or passive voice of the verbs in parentheses. Include the adverb where indicated. Use the simple present, simple past, present continuous, or past continuous tense. In some cases, more than one answer is possible.

THE HISTORY OF COMPUTERS

In 1944, the first general-purpose computer, Mark I, _was put_____ (put) into operation. It was _____1 (be) very slow and very large. In fact, all of the early computers _____2 (be) extremely large, and several floors of a building _____3 (need) to house them.

By the end of the 1950s, computers _____4 (design) to use transistors. Transistors _____5 (make) computers smaller, less expensive, more powerful, and more reliable. Today these _____6 (know) as second-generation computers.

Third-generation computers, which ————————7 (develop) in the 1960s, ————————8 (use) "chips" to store the memory of the computer. These computers ————————9 (be / still) very large, however. When the silicon chip ————————10 (develop) in the early 1970s, computers ————————11 (become) truly small and affordable. Computers with these silicon chips ————————12 (call) fourth-generation computers.

Fourth-generation computers ————————13 (have) tremendous capabilities, but they ————————14 (have / also) limitations. Fifth-generation computers, with artificial intelligence, ————————15 (develop) now. It remains to be seen how the fifth generation will affect our lives.

PART FOUR

Passive Voice — Modal Auxiliaries

LASERS*

Lasers are intense, concentrated beams of light. Today they can be used in surgery, in plane navigation, in supermarket scanners, and in telephone and television transmission. In the near future, our lives may be changed completely by the incredible possibilities of lasers.

---

* *Laser* Light Amplification by Stimulated Emission of Radiation

PASSIVE VOICE—MODAL AUXILIARIES

The passive voice of modal auxiliaries is formed in this way: modal (*can, could, may, might, must, shall, should, will, would*) + *be* + past participle (+ *by* + agent). The passive forms have the same general meanings, functions, and time frames as modal auxiliaries in the active voice. The focus of the sentence shifts, however.

	ACTIVE	PASSIVE
	Today we **can use** lasers in many different fields.	Today lasers **can be used** in many different fields.
Focus:	we	lasers
	A doctor **may use** a laser in an operation.	A laser **may be used** in an operation.
Focus:	a doctor	a laser
	A supermarket **might use** lasers to read food prices.	Lasers **might be used** to read food prices.
Focus:	a supermarket	lasers

■ **EXERCISE A** Complete the following sentences by using the passive forms of the modals and verbs in parentheses.

Example   A laser *may be explained*   (may / explain) by comparing it to ordinary light.

1. Energy _____ (can / store) in any kind of light.

2. The energy in ordinary light _____ (cannot / control) easily.

3. In ordinary light, light waves _____ (may / send) in all directions.

4. On the other hand, laser light _____ (may / focus) on one specific spot.

5. To make a laser, light waves _____ (must / concentrate) in a single direction.

6. The stored energy in a laser ————————— (may / release) in powerful, intense waves.

7. Tremendous heat ————————— (can / produce) by the release of this energy.

8. Much less heat and power ————————— (can / produce) by the energy of ordinary light.

9. A laser beam ————————— (can / control) at many different wavelengths.

10. Different effects ————————— (may / produce) by lasers at each different wavelength.

■ **EXERCISE B** Change the following sentences from the active voice to the passive voice. Omit the agent unless it is important to the meaning of the sentence.

Example   Today people can use lasers in many fields.
          Today lasers can be used in many fields.

1. People can use lasers in filmmaking.
2. In the near future, scientists may employ lasers in many areas of medicine and research.
3. Governments might also put lasers to use in new military applications.
4. Companies will soon use lasers throughout the communications industry.
5. Copper wires can transmit only twenty-four conversations at the same time.
6. Today lasers can transmit 16,000 phone conversations at the same time.
7. In theory, a laser could send the entire text of the Encyclopedia Britannica and the Bible around the earth in less than two seconds.
8. We may never know the full potential of lasers.

■ **EXERCISE C** The following passage is written entirely in the active voice. It contains many sentences that could be improved by using the passive voice. Rewrite the selection using sentences in the passive voice when appropriate. Change at least six verbs. Omit the agent if it is not necessary to the meaning of the sentence.

LASERS AND FIBER OPTICS

In the early part of the century, the telephone revolutionized communications. As the photo here indicates, telephones changed more than communi-

5   cations—they changed the look of our cities. Now, in the last years of the century, lasers and fiber optics are creating another revolution in communications and presenting new challenges.

10   One challenge is how to direct lasers because almost anything may block a laser beam even a cloud, for example, can block a laser beam. As a result, we must direct lasers across an open space, or we must protect them from interference. We can use cables or glass fibers to protect the lasers.

15   We must make these glass fibers from pure glass. Impurities in normal glass will absorb a great deal of light. Thus, we should remove all impurities from the glass in optical fibers for lasers.

Hopefully, we will perfect this technology soon. In the near future, optical fiber systems will replace many copper cables in the communica-

20   tions industry. In fact, optical fiber systems may run all new communications systems of the future. The potential of these systems is tremendous. For example, in theory, a single laser could probably allow half the people in the world to talk to the other half.

PART FIVE

Language Activities

These speaking and writing activities are designed to help you practice the variety of passive verb forms covered in this chapter—with simple, perfect, and continuous tenses and with modal auxiliaries.

SIMPLE PAST TENSE

■ **ACTIVITY A** Have you ever played quiz games like $10,000 Pyramid or Trivial Pursuit? These are question-and-answer games based on categories of information. To play a classroom version, first choose several (five or six) categories from which to draw your questions: music, art, inventions, buildings, discoveries, and so on. Then separate into two groups. In each group, make at least five questions for each category. For example, "Who invented the sewing machine?" or "Name the composer(s) of 'Hey Jude.'" Be sure not to let the other group hear you; they will be asked these questions. After you have completed your questions, give them to your teacher.

Play the game by choosing categories and questions. Points are scored by answering questions correctly. Your teacher will ask each group the questions; a different member of the group must answer each time. You may play until you reach a certain score or until all the questions have been asked. You may also add special rules such as, "An answer must be grammatically correct to score points," or "Five bonus points are given for a correct answer using the passive voice."

CONTRAST OF TENSES

■ **ACTIVITY B** Think of a piece of equipment that is important in your career or in one of your hobbies. When was it invented? By whom? How is it made? How is it used today? What equipment or operations have been developed since the original? Prepare a brief presentation of three to five minutes on this item including pictures and/or a demonstration, if you like. You may present this individually, or in small groups if several students have the same interests.

■ **ACTIVITY C** Imagine that you have the opportunity to interview some "thinking" robots. In small groups, write a short dialogue interviewing one or more robots. Practice the interview and then role-play it for the entire class. Here are some suggested questions to ask. Be sure to add more of your own.

• What are you programmed to do?
• Are you being taught new skills?
• Have you been programmed to smell (see, taste, etc.)?

MODAL AUXILIARIES

■ **ACTIVITY D**   Test your powers of invention. In pairs or in small groups, choose an object. It could be anything—a pencil, a doorknob, a pin. Stare at it and study it carefully. Then tell how the object could be improved. For example, could it be made stronger, smaller, more durable, lighter weight, more attractive, or less expensive?

■ **ACTIVITY E**   In the 1930s, the actor Orson Welles terrified much of the United States when he broadcast H. G. Wells's famous novel *The War of the Worlds* on the radio. Many listeners believed that the story was true. They thought that the earth really was being invaded by Martians with ray guns.

Imagine that the earth is, in fact, being invaded by people from outer space. In small groups, write a short dialogue about this invasion. Try to include as many uses of the passive voice as possible. Then practice your dialogue and role-play it for the entire class.

CHAPTER 4

Money Matters

Nouns, Pronouns, and Noun Modifiers

In this chapter, you will study singular and plural count nouns, noncount nouns, articles, indefinite adjectives and pronouns, and a variety of units of measurement. As you study the chapter, try to understand the distinction between types of nouns in English. This will help you with the use of singular and plural nouns, as well as the use of indefinite and definite articles.

Previewing the Passage

Have you ever taken a course in economics? Do you read or listen to news of the economy? Are you familiar with terms such as *trade, productivity, deficit, interest,* and *debt*? Or is the subject of economics confusing to you?

The Global Economy

Of all the sciences, only two are subjects that have a direct and noticeable effect on our lives every day. One is meteorology, the study of weather. Heat, cold, sun, and rain affect us in many ways—in the kinds of clothing we wear, for example, and the types of activities we do outdoors. Economics is the other
5   science that affects the everyday lives of all of us. Each time we spend money, or it is spent on us, we are contributing to the economic life of our country and, in fact, of the world.

Most people have a basic understanding of the weather, but how many people feel comfortable with the subject of economics? Often economics
10   seems to be a mysterious subject. Newspapers and television use expressions that can resemble a foreign language. They speak of *production* and *consumption*, the *gross national product* (GNP), the *cost of living, productivity,* the *unemployment rate,* the *balance of payments,* and so on.

In some ways, economics is like an enormous jigsaw puzzle. Each piece is
15   basic, but the pieces interconnect, one to another, in a large picture. To look at the whole picture, you must begin piece by piece.

Understanding Vocabulary

Economics is the study of production, distribution, and consumption of goods and services.

1. Which are goods, and which are services?
   a. televisions and stereos
   b. medical checkups
   c. books, paper, pencils, and pens
   d. teaching
   e. clothes
   f. shoes
   g. cars
   h. car repairs
2. Which is an example of production? of distribution? of consumption?
   a. A truck takes furniture to a store.
   b. A family buys a new sofa.
   c. A worker in a factory builds a table.
3. Can you explain any of these economic terms?
   a. gross national product
   b. cost of living
   c. productivity
   d. unemployment rate
   e. balance of payments

Discussing Ideas
1. According to the passage, which sciences affect us every day? Why?
2. Give some examples of economic activities in your daily life.
3. What are other economic terms that you have heard in the news recently? Can you explain them?

PART ONE

Count Nouns and Noncount Nouns, Indefinite Articles

WHAT IS WEALTH TO YOU?

- To some people, wealth may mean ownership of businesses, houses, cars, stereos, and jewels.
- To others, wealth may mean control of resources, such as oil, gold, silver, or natural gas.
- To the philosophical, wealth may be intangible. It can be found in honesty, love, courage, and trust.
- To much of the world, however, wealth is having enough food: bread, rice, fish, meat, and fruit.

COUNT NOUNS

A noun may name a person, a place, an object, an activity, an idea or emotion, or a quantity. Count nouns are nouns that can be counted (*apples, oranges,* etc.). They have both singular and plural forms. Most count nouns are concrete nouns; some are abstract, however. See pages 254–256 for spelling rules for plural nouns and for a list of common irregular plural forms.

Singular	I have a **friend**.
	My friend owns a **car**.
Plural	**Friends** are very important.
	Cars are getting more expensive.

$\longrightarrow$

NONCOUNT NOUNS

Noncount nouns are usually concrete mass nouns (*food, water*, etc.) or abstract nouns (*wealth, happiness*, etc.) that we don't normally count. Noncount nouns are singular, even though some end in *s* (*economics, news*, etc.).

Concrete mass nouns	**Air** and **water** are necessary for life. **Food** is expensive these days. We need to buy **coffee, tea, rice,** and **sugar**.
Abstract nouns	**Honesty** is always best. We need more **information** on that. We're concerned about your **health** and **happiness**. Have you studied **economics** or **physics**?

Noncount nouns often refer to categories or groups. Specific items in these groups are often count nouns.

NONCOUNT	COUNT	NONCOUNT	COUNT
advice	hints ideas suggestions	information and news	articles magazines newspapers
equipment	machines supplies tools	money	cents dollars quarters
friendship and love	feelings friends relatives	nature	animals forests mountains oceans
furniture	chairs lamps tables	time	days hours minutes
homework	assignments essays pages	traffic and transportation	buses cars trains

→

INDEFINITE ARTICLES *A* AND *AN*

| a | I bought **a** banana.
I bought **a** house.
A European man
    lives next door. | *A* is used before a singular count noun that begins
    with a consonant sound. |
| an | I wasted **an** egg.
I wasted **an** hour. | *An* is used before a singular count noun that begins
    with a vowel sound. |

Note: A or *an* is never used with a noun that functions as a noncount noun.

■ **EXERCISE C**   Most people would like to have nice possessions. What would you like? Choose six items from the following list or use ideas of your own. Put your choices in order. Use *a* or *an* with count nouns.

Example   I would like to have (own) . . .
> **First, I would like to own land. Second, I would like to have a large house.**

elegant furniture	land large house	sports car swimming pool
expensive jewelry	nice clothing sailboat	vacation home

■ **EXERCISE D**   What does wealth mean to you? What do you value and why? From the list below, choose six items that are important to you. Put them in order (first, second, and so on). Make count nouns plural and use *are*.

Example   I think . . . is/are (very) important because . . .
> **First, I think good health is important because without health, we have nothing. Second, I think . . .**

accurate
  information
	good health
	good neighbor
		reliable
		  transportation

clean air	homework	respect
courage	honesty	safe housing
elegant clothes	jewelry large family	
expensive car	love	
free time	money in the bank	
friend	peace in the world	

good advice
  from family
  and friends		

Unspecified or Unidentified Count and Noncount Nouns

Both count and noncount nouns may be used to refer to unspecified or unidentified people, things, and so on. In this case, a singular count noun is preceded by *a* or *an*, but plural count nouns and noncount nouns are used without articles.

COUNT NOUNS

Singular **A house** can be expensive.	*a house* = one house or any house in general	Either an article or an adjective *must* be used with a singular count noun.
Plural **Houses** are getting more expensive.	*houses* = all houses in general	Articles are not used with unspecified or unidentified plural count nouns.

NONCOUNT NOUNS

Love is wonderful. **Time** is **money**. **Health** is better than **wealth**.	Articles are not used with unspecified non- count nouns. Noncount nouns always take singular verbs.

■ **EXERCISE E** The following statements include noncount nouns and singular and plural count nouns. Complete each statement by using *a* or *an*, or use *X* to indicate that no article is necessary.

Example I've always been interested in ___*X*___ economics.

I've never taken ___*an*___ economics class.

1. _____ economics is concerned with two basic groups: _____ con-

    sumers and _____ suppliers.

2. _____ economists study the interrelationship between the two groups.

3. For example, _____ economist might study the way _____ supplier

    creates _____ market for _____ new product.

4. _____ economics also deals with the interrelationship between _____ larger groups, including _____ regions and _____ countries.

5. As we all know, _____ change in the economy of _____ country such as Japan can affect _____ people all over the world.

6. Economists study how events in _____ region can affect _____ markets and _____ prices in other regions.

7. For example, _____ weather in California can affect the price of _____ fruit in Boston.

■ **EXERCISE F** The following definitions of economic terms include both count and noncount nouns. Complete the definitions by using *a* or *an*, or use *X* to indicate that no article is necessary.

Example   The balance of _X__ payments is the difference between the amount of _X__ money that leaves _a__ country and the amount that comes in through _X__ imports, _X__ exports, _X__ investments, and so on.

1. _____ *black market* is the illegal sale of _____ products.

2. *Capital* is _____ money or _____ assets such as _____ gold or _____ buildings that can be used to make _____ investments.

3. _____ *depression* is _____ very severe drop in economic activity. _____ high unemployment and _____ low production usually occur during _____ depression.

4. The *gross national product* (*GNP*) is the total value of _____ goods and _____ services produced in _____ country during _____ specified period of _____ time (usually a year).

5. The *money supply* is the total amount of _____ money in circulation.

6. _____ *productivity* is the total national output of _____ goods and _____ services divided by the number of _____ workers.

■ **EXERCISE G** The following sentences make generalizations about large companies. Change the nouns or noun phrases in italics from plural to singular or from singular to plural. Add or omit *a* or *an* and make other changes in verbs and pronouns. (Note that in this exercise, *multinational* and *multinational corporation* have the same meaning.)

Example   *Multinational corporations* are *companies* that operate in more than one country.
A multinational corporation is a company that operates in more than one country.

1. *Multinationals,* such as IBM or Pepsi, may operate in over one hundred countries.
2. Because of their size, *multinational corporations* can often make products at *lower costs* than *local industries* can.
3. *Multinationals* can also make *countries* dependent on them.
4. *A multinational corporation* may import *a raw material* from *a foreign country.*
5. *A multinational* may make *a product* in one country and export it to another country.
6. Today *a country* may require *a company* to build *an assembly plant* in *an area* where *a product* will be sold.
7. Building *a factory* in *a foreign country* can still benefit *a multinational.*
8. It eliminates *a major expense* in transportation.

PART TWO

Indefinite Adjectives and Pronouns

ECONOMICS IN MY LIFE

For many people, economics is a mystery, but I deal with it every day. Economics is just a complicated way of explaining why I make only a little money and why another guy makes a lot of money.

INDEFINITE ADJECTIVES AND PRONOUNS

Indefinite adjectives—such as *some*, *many*, and *little*, are used with nouns instead of giving specific amounts. Indefinite pronouns replace nouns. The type of noun (count or noncount) determines which words may be used.

Indefinite Adjectives and Pronouns with Both Count and Noncount Nouns

	COUNT NOUNS	NONCOUNT NOUNS
any	Do you have **any** dollar bills? I don't have **any** (dollar bills).	Do you have **any** money? I don't have **any** (money).
some	Jack has **some** dollar bills.	Jack has **some** money.
a lot (of) **lot (of)** **plenty (of)**	Henry has **a lot (of** dollar bills).	Henry has **a lot (of** money).
no	I have **no** dollar bills.	I have **no** money.
none	I have **none.**	I have **none.**

■ **EXERCISE A   Oral Practice**   In pairs, ask and answer questions using these cues and words such as *some*, *any*, and *a lot of*. Try to answer truthfully.

Examples   homework tonight
STUDENT A: **Do you have any homework tonight?**
STUDENT B: **Yes, I have some homework.**

money
STUDENT A: **Do you have some money?**
STUDENT B: **No, I don't have any.**

1. extra cash
2. five-dollar bills
3. credit cards
4. interesting news (about . . .)
5. information about good dentists (doctors, therapists, etc.)
6. assignments tonight
7. free time today
8. advice (about . . .)

(*Not*) *Many* Versus (*Not*) *Much, A Few* Versus *A Little*

(*Not*) *many* is used with count nouns. (*Not*) *much* is used with noncount nouns. *Many* and *much* may appear in affirmative statements, but they are more commonly used in negative statements and questions with *How*.

A *few* and *few* are used with count nouns. *A little* and *little* are used with noncount nouns. *Not many* and *not much* are used more frequently than *few* and *little*.

COUNT NOUNS	NONCOUNT NOUNS
How **many** (dollars) do you have?	How **much** (money) do you have?
I have **a few** (dollars). *Meaning:* I have some dollars, but not a lot.	I have **a little** (money). *Meaning:* I have some money, but not a lot.
I **don't** have **many** dollars. *Meaning:* I have only a small number of dollars, probably not enough.	I **don't** have **much** money. *Meaning:* I have only a small amount of money, probably not enough.
I have **few** (dollar bills). *Meaning:* I probably don't have enough.	I have **little** (money). *Meaning:* I probably don't have enough.

Note: Expressions such as *numerous, several,* and *a couple* (*of*) can be used with plural count nouns. Expressions such as *a great deal of* can be used with noncount nouns.

■ **EXERCISE B** *Few* and *little* mean "not many (much)," but *a few* and *a little* mean "some." Indicate the differences in meaning in the following sentences by using + ("some") or − ("not many or much").

Example   + There are a few good restaurants in town.

         − There are few good restaurants in town.

1. _____ We have little homework for the weekend.

2. _____ We have a little homework for the weekend.

3. _____ I have a little advice for you.

4. _____ I have a few ideas for you.

5. _____ He has little information on that.

6. _____ There is little traffic today.

7. _____ Do you have a little time?

8. _____ We have a few pages to read for tomorrow.

9. _____ She has a few friends here.

10. _____ She has few friends here.

11. _____ I've got a little money with me.

12. _____ I've got a few dollars with me.

■ **EXERCISE C Oral Practice**   Take turns making statements and responses following the examples below. Make count nouns plural and use *a little, little, not much, a few, few,* or *not many.*

Examples   money with me
STUDENT A: **I have a little money with me. How about you?**
STUDENT B: **I don't have much money this week.**

dollar with me
STUDENT A: **I have a few dollars with me. How about you?**
STUDENT B: **I have a few dollars too.**

1. free time today
2. furniture in my house (apartment)
3. friend from . . .
4. problem with . . .

5. extra energy
6. homework tonight
7. news from home
8. assignment this week

MODIFIERS WITH *A LOT OF, A LITTLE, A FEW, LITTLE,* AND *FEW*

A lot of, a little, a few, little, and *few* occur frequently in conversation. They are often used with other modifiers. The most common are *quite, just, only, very,* and *too.*

Quite with *A Lot (of)* and *A Few*

COUNT NOUNS	NONCOUNT NOUNS	MEANING
She has **quite a few** assignments.	She has **quite a lot of** homework.	A large number or amount

→

Just and *Only* with *A Few* and *A Little*

COUNT NOUNS	NONCOUNT NOUNS	MEANING
She has **just a few** assignments.	She has **just a little** homework.	a moderate number or amount
She has **only a few** assignments.	She has **only a little** homework.	a small number or amount

Very and *Too* with *Few* and *Little*

COUNT NOUNS	NONCOUNT NOUNS	MEANING
She has **very few** assignments.	She has **very little** homework.	a very small number or amount
She has **too few** assignments.	She has **too little** homework.	not enough

Note: Too can also be used with *many* and *much* to mean "more than enough." Compare the following.

That teacher gives *too many* assignments.
That teacher gives *too much* homework.

■ **EXERCISE D Oral Practice** In pairs, ask and answer questions about your hometown or home country. Use the examples and the following cues. Give your own opinions and offer any additional information you know about the subject. Be sure to make any count nouns plural.

Questions: Is there much (any) . . . ?
Are there many (any) . . . ?

Answers: There is quite a lot (some, just a little, etc.) . . .
There are quite a few (only a few, too few, etc.) . . .

Examples   oil
STUDENT A: **Is there much oil in your country?**
STUDENT B: **Unfortunately, there isn't much oil in my country. We have only a few small oil fields.**

taxi
STUDENT A: **Are there many taxis in Buenos Aires?**
STUDENT B: **There are quite a few — maybe thousands!**

1. gold in . . .
2. tax in . . .
3. poverty
4. crime
5. discrimination
6. air and water pollution
7. farmer
8. factory
9. unemployment
10. news from . . . in U.S. newspapers or on U.S. television

■ **EXERCISE E   Error Analysis**   Many of the following sentences have errors in indefinite pronouns and adjectives. Find and correct the mistakes.

Example   Motor City is a town with many automobile factories.
              many
How ~~much~~ factories are there in Motor City?

1. I've worked at Mass Production Motors for a few years.
2. We have a lot problems in this factory.
3. The workers are paid very few money.
4. We don't get no job satisfaction here.
5. There are too much unhappy workers in this factory.
6. Only a little people are happy with their jobs.
7. Last year there weren't much strikes, but this year we're going to have plenty of.
8. So far we haven't had much success in changing things.
9. The management has tried to make some changes, but it's had very little success.
10. Many of workers are against the changes.

PART THREE

The Definite Article with Count and Noncount Nouns

WORLD RESOURCES: WHERE ARE THEY?

Some of the world's most important resources are coal, iron ore, petroleum, copper, gold, silver, and diamonds. Many deposits are concentrated in small areas, such as the petroleum deposits off the coast of Venezuela and in the deserts around the Persian Gulf.

THE DEFINITE ARTICLE WITH COUNT NOUNS

The is used before a singular or plural count noun when that noun is specifically identified or its identity is already understood.

	SINGULAR	PLURAL
Nonspecific (**without** *the*)	Today **a company** may earn over one billion dollars annually.	Today **companies** may earn over one billion dollars annually.
Specific (with *the*)	**The company** with the highest income is Exxon.	Today **the companies** that earn over one billion dollars annually are primarily oil companies.

$\longrightarrow$

Identified or Specified Nouns

Unique nouns	Many of the largest companies in **the world** are oil companies. Oil companies control most of **the earth's** known oil reserves.	*The* is used with names of people, places, and so on, that are considered to be one of a kind. These include *the earth, the world, the moon, the sun, the universe; the president* and *the pope.* Exception: *on earth*
Repeated nouns	He works for **an oil company. The company** has sent him to work in many different parts of the country. He enjoys working for **the company,** but he is tired of traveling.	After a noun has been mentioned once, *the* is used with later references to that noun.
Phrases	**The majority of companies** with billion-dollar incomes are oil companies.	Phrases that come immediately after a noun often identify it, so *the* is used. *The* + noun + *of* is a frequent combination.
Clauses	Today **the companies that earn over one billion dollars** are oil companies.	Like phrases, clauses may identify or specify *which* person, place, or thing.
Superlatives and ordinal numbers	The company with **the highest income** is Exxon.	*The* is normally used with superlatives (*the most, the least*) and ordinal numbers (*the first*).

■ **EXERCISE A** The following sentences include both specific and non-specific count nouns. Complete them by using *the,* or use *X* to indicate that no article is necessary.

Example   _X_   natural resources are important to all countries.

1. _____ most important resources in England are tin and iron ore.

2. _____ raw materials are used to make _____ products.

3. _____ raw materials that are used to make _____ cars include iron ore, rubber, and petroleum.

4. _____ petroleum deposits are located in many parts of the world.

5. _____ petroleum deposits in the Amazon will be difficult to extract.

6. _____ mines can be _____ very dangerous places to work.

7. _____ mines near Bogotá, Colombia, produce large quantities of salt.

8. _____ coal mines in West Virginia have caused many deaths.

THE DEFINITE ARTICLE WITH NONCOUNT NOUNS

Articles are not generally used with noncount nouns. However, noncount nouns, like count nouns, may be preceded by *the* when the noun is *specifically identified*.

| **Nonspecific** (without *the*)
 Specific (with *the*) | **Gold** is a precious metal.

 The gold in jewelry is mixed with other metals.
 The gold that is used in jewelry is mixed with other metals.
 South Africa produces **the most gold** in the world. | No articles are used with unspecified nouns.

 The is used with a non-count noun when the noun is identified by a phrase or clause.

 The is usually used with superlatives. |

■ **EXERCISE B** The following sentences include both specific and non-specific noncount nouns. Complete them by using *the,* or use *X* to indicate that no article is necessary.

Example   _X_   silver is valuable.

1. Most of _____ silver in the United States is used to make photographic and X-ray film.

2. _____ iron ore is used to make _____ steel.

3. _____ iron ore from eastern Canada is high in quality.

4. Japan produces some of _____ best steel in the world today.

5. _____ oil from Saudi Arabia is lighter in weight than _____ oil from Venezuela.

6. _____ oil is the most important single factor in the world's economy.

7. _____ gold is perhaps _____ most highly treasured metal.

8. Since 1910, one-third of _____ gold in the world has been mined in South Africa.

THE WITH PROPER NOUNS

The has specific uses with proper nouns, especially with geographical locations. Because proper nouns identify specific places, *the* is often used. There are few exceptions to the rules. Study the chart on pages 262 and 263 and use it for reference.

■ **EXERCISE C   Oral Practice**   Use *the* or *X* with the following phrases.

Example   *the* Hawaiian Islands

       X   Hawaii

1. _____ Great Lakes

2. _____ Lake Superior

3. _____ America

4. _____ United States

5. _____ Golden Gate Bridge

6. _____ equator

7. _____ Saudi Arabia

8. _____ 1995

9. _____ 1990s

10. _____ Philippine Islands

11. _____ Museum of Modern Art

12. _____ Rocky Mountains

13. _____ earth

14. _____ Canada

15. _____ president

16. _____ President Kennedy

17. _____ University of California

18. _____ Harvard University

19. _____ eighteenth of March

20. _____ Japanese (people)

■ **EXERCISE D** Complete the following sentences by using *the*, or use *X* to indicate that no article is necessary.

1. The world's major source of diamonds is **_X_** southern Africa. _____ Star of _____ Africa, the world's largest cut diamond, was found there. Today _____ Star of _____ Africa is one of _____ British crown jewels kept in _____ Tower of _____ London.

2. The world's finest emeralds are mined in _____ Andes Mountains in _____ Colombia, _____ South America. The most important mine is located near _____ town of _____ Muzo on _____ Minero River.

3. The world's largest rock crystal, one thousand pounds, was found in _____ Burma. A piece of this rock crystal is displayed at _____ National Museum in _____ Washington, D.C.

4. The largest known pearl was found in _____ Philippine Islands in _____ 1930s. It weighed fourteen pounds, one ounce. The largest known black pearl was found near _____ Fiji in _____ 1984.

5. _____ world's largest gold mine is in _____ South Africa. _____ South Africa supplies 60 percent to 70 percent of _____ gold in _____ world. _____ largest uranium field in _____ world is also located in _____ South Africa.

■ **EXERCISE E** Make complete sentences from the following cues. Add *of*, *from*, and *in* and be sure to include *the* when necessary.

Example   large gold deposits / exist / Andes Mountains / South America
Large gold deposits exist in the Andes Mountains in South America.

1. oil / be a valuable resource
2. oil / Saudi Arabia / be lightweight and high in quality
3. copper / South America / be easy to mine
4. copper / be important for the communications industry
5. silver / United States / be primarily found / Rocky Mountains
6. silver / be used to make photographic film
7. 40 percent / silver / United States / be used for photography
8. diamonds / be / precious gems
9. large diamond mines / exist / Ural Mountains / Soviet Union
10. 25 percent / diamonds / world / be found / West Africa

■ **EXERCISE F**   Complete the following by adding *the*, or use *X* to indicate that no article is necessary.

WHERE MINERALS ARE LOCATED

Some of _*the*_ earth's most valuable resources are found in only a few
countries. For example, _____₁ South Africa and _____₂ Soviet Union produce one-third to one-half of many vital resources. They are _____₃ world's
largest producers of _____₄ manganese, _____₅ chrome, _____₆ platinum,
and _____₇ gold. _____₈ Australia is another country that contains major
resources. It has large deposits of _____₉ oil, _____₁₀ gas, _____₁₁ iron ore,
and _____₁₂ coal. In fact, _____₁₃ Japan gets almost one-half of its iron ore
(which is used to make _____₁₄ steel) and _____₁₅ large quantities of its coal
from _____₁₆ Australia. _____₁₇ Canada, too, has _____₁₈ large mineral
deposits. _____₁₉ oil and _____₂₀ natural gas deposits in _____₂₁ Canada are
some of _____₂₂ biggest in the world.

PART FOUR

Units of Measurement

HOW DO YOU SPEND YOUR FOOD DOLLARS?

In 1940, Americans consumed 19.4 pounds
of butter and margarine per person, and
most of this was butter. Now they eat less
than 16 pounds, mostly margarine.

UNITS OF MEASUREMENT

Units of measurement are commonly used in this pattern: number or percentage + unit + *of* + name of item.

UNIT OF MEASUREMENT	ITEMS
bar	hand soap, candy
bottle	liquids such as beer, soda pop, and wine
box	solids such as cereal and crackers
bunch	items that grow together—such as bananas, celery, or grapes—and items that are tied together, such as flowers. In informal English, *a bunch* is often used to mean "a lot."
can	liquids and solids such as soda pop, beer, and vegetables
carton	eggs; milk, ice cream, and other dairy products; cigarettes
dozen, half dozen	eggs; cookies, rolls, and other items bought in quantities of six or twelve (*Note: Of* is not used with *dozen* or *half dozen.*)
gallon, quart, pint, ounce	most liquids and ice cream
head	lettuce, cabbage, cauliflower
jar	jam, mayonnaise, and other items that are spread with a knife
loaf	bread
piece, slice	most solids, such as bread, cake, cheese, and meat
pound, ounce	cheese, butter, fruit, meat, poultry, and other solids
roll	paper towels, toilet paper
six-(twelve-)pack	soda pop and beer
tube	toothpaste, creams

■ **EXERCISE A** Complete the following grocery lists by adding appropriate units of measurement. Be sure to use *of* when necessary.

2 *pounds of* ground beef   1 _____ grapes

1 _____ butter   1 _____ crackers

1 _____ milk   1 _____ mayonnaise

1 _____ eggs   5 _____ hand soap

1 _____ lettuce		1 _____ toothpaste
3 _____ cereal		1 _____ wine
2 _____ paper towels		1 _____ ice cream
1 _____ jam		3 _____ bread
1 _____ bananas		1 _____ celery
1 _____ soda pop		2 _____ cheese

■ **YOUR TURN** Are you going grocery shopping soon? Make a list of at least six items that you need to buy. Use appropriate units of measurement.

■ **EXERCISE B** Using the following chart of equivalents, convert the following amounts from metric to British units. You may give approximate (rounded-off) equivalents.

Example   four liters of milk
Four liters of milk are approximately equal to one gallon of milk.

1. one liter of milk
2. three meters of fabric
3. thirty-two liters of gas
4. ten centimeters of tape

5. three kilograms of cheese
6. a meter of rope
7. ten milliliters of sugar
8. twenty degrees Celsius

METRIC AND BRITISH UNITS

Length	Meter: about 1.1 yards (3 feet = 1 yard) Centimeter: .01 meter; about .4 inch Kilometer: 1,000 meters; about .6 mile
Volume	Liter: about 1.06 quarts or 2.1 pints Milliliter: 0.001 liter; five make a teaspoon
Weight	Gram: 30 = 1.1 ounces Kilogram: 1,000 grams; about 2.2 pounds
Temperature	Celsius: $0°C = 32°F$

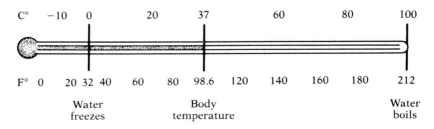

C°	−10	0	20	37	60	80	100

F°	0	20 32 40	60	80	98.6	120	140	160	180	212

Water freezes   Body temperature   Water boils

■ **EXERCISE C**   Use the chart of equivalents again. This time convert the following amounts from British to metric units. You may give approximate (rounded-off) equivalents.

Example   four gallons of gas
          Four gallons of gas is approximately equal to sixteen liters of gas.

1. two pounds of cheese
2. one quart of milk
3. five pounds of chicken
4. two yards of fabric
5. one teaspoon of salt
6. ten feet of rope
7. three inches of string
8. three teaspoons of sugar

■ **EXERCISE D   Review of Articles**   Complete the next passage by using *a*, *an*, or *the*, or by using *X* to indicate that no article is necessary. Explain any cases where you feel more than one choice may be appropriate.

THE GREEN REVOLUTION

In 1910, _X_ farmers represented 33 percent of _the_ U.S. work force, and it took more than ____₁ hour of ____₂ work to produce ____₃ bushel of ____₄ corn. By 1980, two minutes of ____₅ work produced ____₆ same amount, and ____₇ farm employment had fallen to about 3 percent.

In 1950, ____₈ very good dairy cow could produce 1,200 gallons of ____₉ milk per year. By 1987, ____₁₀ dairy cows were averaging 2,400 gallons ____₁₁ year, and some prize cows had even reached 6,000 gallons. During ____₁₂ 1990s, ____₁₃ milk production is expected to increase by at least 15 to 20 percent.

These are only two examples of ____₁₄ dramatic changes that have occurred in ____₁₅ agriculture. Through ____₁₆ advances in ____₁₇ science and ____₁₈ technology, ____₁₉ modern agriculture has become one of ____₂₀ greatest success stories of this century.

Yet despite the "green revolution," ____₂₁ hunger plagues ____₂₂ earth. According to ____₂₃ World Bank, at least 730 million people are malnourished — so poorly fed that they are unable to lead ____₂₄ normal, active lives — and, unfortunately, ____₂₅ number of ____₂₆ malnourished people will continue to rise as ____₂₇ 85 million babies are born each year. We need _____28 annual food increase equal to _____29 Canada's total yearly grain harvest just to keep up with _____30 growth in _____31 population worldwide.

Language Activities

These speaking and writing activities are designed to help you practice using nouns with and without articles or adjectives.

NOUNS WITHOUT ARTICLES — GENERALIZATIONS

■ **ACTIVITY A**   A *generalization* is a general statement that expresses an idea or an opinion about people, things, ideas, and so on. It often gives a general rule or conclusion based on limited or insufficient information. For example, consider these statements. Are they always true?

1. French people drink wine.
2. Japanese people always have dark hair.
3. American men are tall.
4. Latin Americans are fantastic dancers.

Note that these generalizations use nouns without articles. This is one of the most common ways to make generalizations. As a class or in small groups, share some of the generalizations that are common in your culture. Include both generalizations that people in your culture make and generalizations that others make about people in your culture.

COUNT AND NONCOUNT NOUNS — RESOURCES

■ **ACTIVITY B**   Are you interested in knowing more about gold? petroleum? diamonds? a certain kind of wood — mahogany, teak, ebony? a certain kind of rock — marble, slate, granite? Choose one resource that you would like to learn more about and briefly research it at a library. Gather information on where this resource is found today, how it is extracted, and how it is used. Use your research as the basis for a short composition. Finally, share your information with the rest of the class in a three- to five-minute presentation.

COUNT AND NONCOUNT NOUNS—FOOD

■ **ACTIVITY C** Work in pairs. Imagine that your partner has offered to go grocery shopping for you. Dictate a list to your partner of at least eight items that you need to buy. Then change roles.

Example   I need two dozen eggs, a gallon of milk, . . .

■ **ACTIVITY D** Go around the room in a chain drill, listing items you need to buy. The first student tells one item. The second student must repeat that item and add one. Continue with each student repeating the list and adding one item.

Example   STUDENT A: **two dozen eggs**
STUDENT B: **two dozen eggs and a gallon of milk**
STUDENT C: **two dozen eggs, a gallon of milk, and . . .**

■ **ACTIVITY E** In small groups, discuss household staples and daily necessities in your countries or cultures; include common household items as well as food. Compare changes that have occurred in recent years, including changes in diet or use and in price. Use a chart like the one below to help you.

You may separate into groups from the same region, country, or culture. Then, as a class, compare the differences from group to group. Or, if possible, include representatives of various countries and cultures in each group. Compare the differences within each group.

COUNTRY OR CULTURE	ITEM	COMMENTS
Colombia	Bread vs. <u>Arepas</u>	Arepas are made of corn produced in Colombia. They used to be a staple food, and a family would consume dozens of them a day. This has changed a lot. Now Colombians buy loaves of bread made of flour that has been imported.

CHAPTER 5

Leisure Time

Gerunds, Infinitives, and Other Verb Forms

In this chapter, you will study the use of infinitives and gerunds, including how they can function as nouns, which verbs they often follow, and how the use of one or the other can change the meaning of a sentence. You will also look at a few uses of other verb forms—simple, present participle, and past participle forms.

115

Previewing the Passage

Do you lead a fast-paced life, or do you have a lot of spare time? Is taking time to relax an important part of your life?

How Important Is Leisure Time?

How important is leisure time? How important is free time to relax and to collect yourself? Many doctors believe that learning to relax in order to relieve day-to-day tension could one day save your life.

5   In our fast-paced world, it is almost impossible to avoid building up tension from stress. All of us confront stress daily; anything that places an extra demand on us causes stress. We encounter stress on the job, and we face it at home.

The body responds to stress by mobilizing its defenses. Blood pressure rises, and muscles get ready to act. If our tension is not relieved, it can start
10   numerous reactions, both physical and psychological. Yet we can learn to cope with stress effectively and to avoid its consequences. How? By relaxing in the face of stress. According to researcher Hans Selye of the University of Montreal, the effects of stress depend not on what happens to us but on the way we react. In times of stress, taking a few moments to sit quietly and relax can make
15   anyone feel better.

Understanding Vocabulary

1. Which does *not* belong?
   a. free time
   b. stress
   c. spare time
   d. leisure time
   e. relaxation
2. The word *stress* has several meanings. What kind of stress is discussed in the passage?
   a. force or pressure that strains or deforms something
   b. mental or physical tension
   c. emphasis or importance
   d. emphasis on a word or syllable

Discussing Ideas

1. According to the passage, what causes stress?
2. How does the body react physically to stress?
3. According to the passage, what is the best way to cope with stress?

Forms of Gerunds and Infinitives; Prepositions Followed by Gerunds; Adjectives, Adverbs, and Nouns Followed by Infinitives

TO EACH HIS OWN

For some people, listening to classical music is fun, but it's really difficult for me to sit through a whole concert. Now rock music — that's another story!

GERUNDS

Gerunds have the same forms as present participles (simple form + -*ing*), but they are used as nouns.

Noun object of a verb	I enjoy **the ocean.**
Gerund object of a verb	I enjoy **swimming.**
Gerund subject	**Swimming** is my favorite sport.
Gerund complement	My favorite sport is **swimming.**
Gerund object of a preposition	By **swimming** every day, I can get a lot of exercise.

$\longrightarrow$

Active Versus Passive Gerunds

Passive gerunds are formed by using *being* and the past participle of the main verb. *Not* is used before the gerund to form the negative. Possessive nouns or pronouns may also be used before gerunds.

ACTIVE	PASSIVE
Losing a job is difficult.	**Being fired** can often be a terrible experience.
Not having a job can be difficult.	**Not being rehired** is almost like being fired.
Everyone was worried about **John's (his) finding** a job.	Everyone was concerned about **Miki's (her) being fired.**

Gerunds as Objects of Prepositions

Only the gerund form of verbs may be used to replace nouns as the objects of prepositions.

Noun object of a preposition	Thanks **for the phone call.** Thanks **for the invitation.**
Gerund object of a preposition	Thanks **for calling.** Thanks **for inviting** us.

Common Expressions with Prepositions That Are Often Followed by Gerunds

be accused of	be satisfied with (dissatisfied with)	plan on
be afraid of	be tired of	put off
be famous for	approve of (disapprove of)	talk about (talk over)
be fed up with	blame (praise) someone for	think about
be good at	complain about	worry about
be interested in	excuse someone for	How about . . . ?
	get through	

$\longrightarrow$

Expressions with *to* That Are Often Followed by Gerunds

In the following idiomatic expressions, *to* is a preposition, and the gerund form follows it if a verb form is used. Do not confuse the preposition *to* with the *to* used in infinitives (*to* + verb).

Noun object of *to*	I am looking forward **to the party.**	be accustomed to be opposed to
Gerund object of *to*	**I am looking forward to seeing you.** (*Not* I am looking forward to see you.)	be subjected to be used to look forward to object to plead guilty (innocent) to

■ **EXERCISE A Forms of Gerunds** Complete the following sentences with active or passive gerunds formed from the verbs in parentheses. Include negatives and possessives when indicated.

LAUGHTER AND RELAXATION

Example *Laughing*_____ (laugh) is one of the healthiest

ways of *relaxing*_____ (relax).

1. _____ (laugh) can keep you from

   _____ (worry) about a problem.

2. Some humor is universal, but other humor depends on

   _____ (you / understand) certain types of jokes.

3. _____ (understand / not) American humor is a

   problem for many foreigners.

4. People everywhere enjoy _____ (listen) to jokes.

   In fact, some people don't even mind _____

   (tell) the same joke several times.

5. _____ (make) people laugh can be a full-time

   job. For example, comedians and circus clowns earn their living by

   _____ (laugh) at.

■ **EXERCISE B** **Prepositions Followed by Gerunds** Complete the following conversations by adding prepositions and forming gerunds from the verbs below. Use each verb and each preposition at least once.

be	hear	✓ watch	in
become	✓ listen	write	of
get	lose	about	on
go	see	at	to
have	take	for	with

1. JOHN: I'm tired _of_____ _watching_____ television. Let's find
   something else to do.
   SUSAN: Well, the news will be on the radio in a minute. Are you
   interested _in_____ _listening_____ to it?
   JOHN: No, I'm not. I'm fed up _____ _____ only
   bad news.
   SUSAN: If you want to change things, how _____
   _____ a news reporter? You're good _____
   _____ stories. Then you could tell about good news!

2. NANCY: You look upset. What's the matter?
   SANDY: Jim is afraid _____ _____ his job. He's
   worried _____ _____ fired.
   NANCY: You both need some rest and relaxation. Why don't you
   think _____ _____ a short trip this weekend?
   I know a place that is famous _____ _____ very
   relaxing.

3. FRED: Aren't you looking forward _____ _____ to
   the movies tonight?
   MARGARET: I like movies, but the movie you are planning
   _____ _____ is very violent.
   FRED: Well, would you object _____ _____ dinner at a restaurant instead?

■ **EXERCISE C   Prepositions Followed by Gerunds**   Do you have a hobby, sport, or some other activity that you enjoy? Use this exercise to tell your classmates about it.

Complete the following sentences by using gerunds after the prepositions and by adding any other necessary information. You may want to use the verbs *do, watch, listen* (*to*), *try, study,* and *buy.*

Example   Some people can learn . . . by . . .
   Some people can learn photography by studying it.

1. Some people learn best by . . .
2. Other people learn from . . . others.
3. Here are my recommendations for . . .
4. You should start by . . .
5. Before . . . , you should . . .
6. While . . . , you should . . .
7. Instead of . . . , you should . . .
8. After . . . , you . . .

INFINITIVES

The infinitive is *to* + the simple form of the verb. Like the gerund, it is a verb form that can replace a noun in a sentence. It may *not* be the object of a preposition, however. In addition, an infinitive (or *in order* + infinitive) may be used as a modifier to show purpose. In this use, it may appear at various points within a sentence.

Noun object of a verb	I would like **dinner.**
Infinitive object of a verb	I would like **to eat.**
Infinitive complement	His favorite pastime is **to eat** in nice restaurants.
Infinitive subject	**To eat** at Maxim's is one of his goals.
Anticipatory *it* as the subject before an infinitive	**It** is expensive **to eat** there.
Infinitive of purpose	**To pay** the bill, he'll save for a month. He'll have to save for a month (**in order**) **to pay** the bill.

Note: When two or more infinitives appear in a series, it is not necessary to repeat *to.* Compare the following.

He loves **to eat, to drink,** and **to be** merry.
He loves **to eat, drink,** and **be** merry.

$\longrightarrow$

Active Versus Passive Infinitives

Passive infinitives are formed by using *to be* + the past participle of the main verb. *Not* is used before the infinitive to form the negative. *For* + a noun or object pronoun often precedes the infinitive as its subject.

ACTIVE	PASSIVE
We wanted **to tell** John about the plans.	John has **to be told** about the plans.
Mary said **not to tell** him.	There is no reason for him **not to be told.**
It's important **for him to know** about this.	It's important **for John to be told.**

ADVERBS, ADJECTIVES, AND NOUNS FOLLOWED BY INFINITIVES

ADVERBS

too	This tennis racket is **too** heavy for me **to use.**	*Too* often implies a negative result: *This racket is very heavy; I can't use it.*
not . . . enough	This handle isn't big **enough to grip** well.	*Not enough* also implies a negative result: *This handle isn't very big, so I can't grip it well.*
enough	This racket is light **enough to use** yet strong **enough to last** a long time.	*Enough* implies a positive result: *This racket is very light, but it will also last a long time.*
how what when where	I would like to learn **how to play** tennis well. I would like to know **where to buy** a good racket.	Phrases with *what, when, where,* and *how* are reduced forms of noun clauses: *I would like to learn how I can play tennis well. I would like to know where I can buy a good racket.*

⟶

ADJECTIVES

I am **pleased to see** you. It is **great to see** you.	Many adjective / infinitive combinations follow this pattern: *It + be + adjective + infinitive*.
It was **nice of you to come**.	*Of* + an object often follows adjectives such as *nice, good*, and *polite*.
He was **the first** (person) **to leave**.	Infinitives often follow ordinals (*the first, the second*, etc.) or adjectives such as *the last* and *the only*.

NOUNS

Is this a good time **to visit** them? That would be a nice thing **to do**. It's a beautiful place **to visit**. **In order to finish**, we have to work faster. (**To finish**, we have to work faster.)	Infinitives are often used in the following combination: *This / That / It + be + adjective + noun + infinitive*. Infinitives are also used to express purpose or goals. *In order* is not necessary for this meaning; it may be omitted.
There is work **to be done**. I have work **to do**. She wants a magazine **to read**. Do you have money **to buy** one? We'll find a way **to get** one.	Similarly, infinitives can be used after nouns to show what should or can be done with the nouns. *There + be + noun + infinitive* is a common combination.

■ **EXERCISE D** Gerunds are used more often than infinitives as subjects of sentences. However, infinitives are frequently used with anticipatory *it* as a subject. Change the following sentences to begin with *It*.

Example Listening to music is relaxing.
It's relaxing to listen to music.

1. For many people, hearing classical music is enjoyable.
2. For other people, going to a rock concert is more fun.
3. Playing classical music well can be difficult.
4. Learning a piece of music can take several weeks.
5. Appreciating classical music has never (always) been easy for me.

■ **EXERCISE E Forms of Infinitives** Complete the following by using either active or passive infinitive forms of the verbs in parentheses. Be sure to include negatives or subjects (phrases with *for*) when indicated.

STRESS

LOIS: What a stressful day! I need *to take* _____ (take) a

vacation!

CLARK: You certainly look tired. It would be good

for you to get away _____ (you / get away) for a while.

LOIS: This story had _____₁ (finish) by 10:00 A.M.

In order _____₂ (I / finish) it on time, I had

_____₃ (stay) up all last night. It would be

terrific _____₄ (have / not)

_____₅ (work) for the rest of the day.

CLARK: Wouldn't it be great _____₆ (take) a month

off? It would be nice _____₇ (do) nothing

but relax.

LOIS: It would be even nicer _____₈ (the boss /

give) us a raise. Then I wouldn't need

_____₉ (work) so much. Well, it's easy

_____₁₀ (dream), isn't it?

■ **YOUR TURN** Form complete sentences from the following and add a few of your own.

1. It's hard . . .
2. It's easy for me . . .
3. It's fun . . .

4. It's interesting . . .
5. It's boring . . .

■ **EXERCISE F** Add infinitive phrases to complete the following.

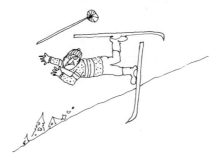

Example I'm interested in learning how _to ski_____.

1. I'm looking for a pair of skis. Can you tell me where . . . ?
2. Have you considered classes? It would be a good idea . . .
3. Many beginners have a hard time because skiing is a difficult sport . . .
4. It usually takes several years . . .
5. Where can I get skis? Do you know of a good place . . .
6. I don't want to go alone. Do you have time . . . ?
7. I don't know anything about skis. Can you tell me what . . . ?
8. You can always rent skis if you don't have enough money . . .
9. Can you tell me where I can rent skis? I don't know where . . .
10. Thanks for your time. It was really nice of you . . .

■ **EXERCISE G** Complete the following passages by filling in the gerund or the infinitive forms (active or passive) of the verbs in parentheses. Be sure to include negatives or subjects (_for_ + noun / pronoun) when indicated.

1. **Learning to Relax**

   _Relaxing_____ (relax) should be easy, but many people

   are accustomed to _____₁ (keep up) a fast pace

   in their work, and it is difficult _____₂ (they /

   relax). Instead of _____₃ (enjoy) a free moment,

   they immediately worry about _____₄ (do)

   something else.

2. **Yoga**

   Interest in _____₅ (learn) yoga is very high and

   with good reason. Millions of people have begun to realize the

   effects of _____₆ (live) with stress and the importance

   of _____₇ (relax). Yoga is a discipline that combines

   mental, spiritual, and physical well-being. It teaches you how

   _____₈ (care) for your health and beauty at the

   same time. Most yoga exercises consist of _____₉

   (stretch) your body while breathing regularly and deeply. By

   _____₁₀ (practice) disciplines such as yoga, you

   can learn how _____₁₁ (slow) yourself down and

   _____₁₂ (appreciate) the effects of relaxation.

P A R T   T W O

Verbs Followed by Gerunds or Infinitives

THE SKY ABOVE US

Humans have always been fascinated by the sky, the wind, and the stars. Even in ancient times, men and women imagined flying or traveling through space. And some of the world's greatest inventions — telescopes, airplanes, satellites — have come from people who hoped to master the heavens.

VERBS FOLLOWED BY GERUNDS OR INFINITIVES

Some verbs may be followed by gerunds, some by infinitives, and some by either. See pages 254–267 for a complete list of verbs followed by gerunds or infinitives with examples.

Verbs Followed by Gerunds

I **can't help wondering** about the universe.
Can you **imagine traveling** through outer space?

anticipate	imagine
be worth	involve
can(not) help	mind
consider	recommend
enjoy	suggest

Verbs Followed by Infinitives

Would you **dare to try** skydiving?
I **would like to learn how to hang-glide.**

appear	know how
be	learn (how)
be able	need*
be supposed	plan
dare*	seem
decide	want*
have	would like*
hope	would love*

---

* More information on these verbs is given in Part Three.

■ **EXERCISE A** Complete the following using gerund or infinitive forms of the verbs in parentheses.

Example   They appeared . . . (be angry)
They appeared to be angry.

1. We anticipated . . . (get home late)
2. It was worth . . . (wait for him)
3. We decided . . . (leave earlier)
4. She enjoyed . . . (visit Hawaii)
5. He didn't mind . . . (tell about that) (passive)
6. He needed . . . (tell about that) (passive)
7. They recommended . . . (see a doctor)
8. I would like . . . (see her)

■ **EXERCISE B** Form complete sentences from the following cues.

Example   want / study
He wanted to study medicine.

1. appear / be
2. decide / stay
3. enjoy / listen
4. hope / return
5. not mind / help
6. plan / study
7. want / learn
8. would like / visit

■ **EXERCISE C** Rephrase each sentence using the cues below. Pay attention to the use of infinitives and gerunds.

Example   Would you enjoy flying a plane?
Would you dare **to fly a plane?**
Can you imagine **flying a plane?**

1. Do you want to learn how to fly a plane?
   Would you like . . .
2. You need to find a good instructor.
   I recommend . . .
3. I hope to begin flight classes soon.
   I anticipate . . .
4. Becoming a pilot involves spending a lot of money.
   Someone who is becoming a pilot has . . .
5. Some student pilots decide to buy a plane.
   Some student pilots are able . . .
6. My instructor wants to rent a plane.
   My instructor suggests . . .

■ **EXERCISE D** Complete the following using gerund or infinitive forms of the verbs in parentheses. Be sure to include negatives, possessives, or subjects when indicated.

AMATEUR ASTRONOMY

1. Would you like *to know* _____ (know) more about the stars but don't know where _____ (begin)? Well, even though there appear _____ (be) millions of stars, only about six thousand are visible.

2. The visible stars are the brightest but not necessarily the closest. Many of these seem _____ (group) together. These groupings are called constellations, and many have unusual names, such as Taurus the Bull and Orion the Hunter. You can learn _____ (recognize) many of the constellations by _____ (remember) what they represent.

3. The best time for _____ (you / study) the stars is during cold, clear nights. It is easier _____ (see) many of the fainter stars then because the atmosphere lets more light reach the earth.

4. Don't be discouraged by _____ (have / not) a telescope. You can always see important stars — like Polaris, the North Star. Early navigators knew how _____ (tell) direction by _____ (find) Polaris because it is almost directly over the North Pole. In order _____ (keep) a steady direction east or west, you have _____ (make) sure Polaris is in the same position each night. Explorers have used this method of _____ (navigate) for over three thousand years.

5. If you are interested in _____ (learn) more, consider _____ (enroll) in a course or

_____ (join) a local group of astronomers. And, of course, before _____ (invest) in a telescope or any expensive equipment, ask your local science museum or school department for advice.

■ **EXERCISE E**   Complete the following, using gerund or infinitive forms of the verbs in parentheses. Be sure to include subjects when indicated.

BIRD-WATCHING

There are some things you can do anywhere — like observing birds. Bird-_watching_ (watch) is a pastime, even a competitive sport, for millions of people around the world. To bird lovers, it's thrilling _____₁ (see) a rare bird in the wild, but it's equally exciting _____₂ (observe) birds close to home. The sport is a relaxing but rewarding one for anyone who enjoys _____₃ (be) outdoors. Bird-watchers recommend _____₄ (you / buy) a guidebook to local birds and _____₅ (get) good, comfortable shoes for _____₆ (walk). They suggest _____₇ (visit) your local parks regularly and perhaps _____₈ (get) involved in a bird-watching society. Within a short time, you will learn _____₉ (identify) many species of birds.

PART THREE

More Verbs Followed by Gerunds or Infinitives

THE GREAT OUTDOORS

Some people spend their time relaxing indoors, but other people need to get outside and do things. It's easy if you happen to live in a sunny place like Florida!

MORE VERBS THAT ARE FOLLOWED BY GERUNDS

I **appreciated** your **explaining** the rules.
You should **spend** some **time reading** the rule book.

admit	finish	regret
appreciate	forgive	risk
avoid	keep (on)	spend (time)
delay	miss	tolerate
dislike	postpone	understand
escape	practice	

MORE VERBS THAT ARE FOLLOWED BY INFINITIVES

Can you **afford to buy** that new set of golf clubs?
I would **hesitate to spend** that much money.

afford	hesitate	refuse
agree	intend	tend
care	manage	threaten
deserve	mean	volunteer
fail	offer	wait
forget	prepare	wish
happen	pretend	

■ **EXERCISE A** Complete the following using gerund or infinitive forms of the verbs in parentheses. Be sure to include negatives and make other changes when indicated.

Example   We can't afford . . . (buy that car)
We can't afford to buy that car.

1. They agreed . . . (not / tell anyone)
2. We appreciated . . . (he / tell us that)
3. He had avoided . . . (tell us)
4. She deserved . . . (tell) (passive)
5. I can't forgive . . . (they / not / tell us)
6. He happened . . . (mention / the subject)
7. We regretted . . . (not / tell) (passive)
8. He waited . . . (tell / officially) (passive)

■ **EXERCISE B** Rephrase each sentence using the cues below. Pay attention to the use of infinitives and gerunds.

Example   When I was younger, I managed to play soccer almost every day.
When I was younger, I spent time **playing soccer almost every day.**

1. I miss having time to play soccer. I regret not . . .
2. There happens to be a soccer game this afternoon. Would you care . . . ?
3. I meant to tell you about the game sooner. I intended . . .
4. Let's avoid spending a lot of money. I can't afford . . .
5. John has volunteered to buy the tickets. John has offered . . .
6. They'll delay playing the game if it rains. They'll postpone . . .

Verbs That May Be Followed by a Noun or Pronoun Object Before an Infinitive

Infinitives may follow these verbs directly, or a noun or pronoun object may come between the verb and the infinitive. The meaning of the sentence changes with the use of a noun or pronoun. Note that *for* is not used before the noun or pronoun.

Verb + (noun or pronoun) + infinitive	She **asked to play** soccer with us.	ask	promise
	She **asked her friend to play** soccer with us.	beg	want
		dare	would like
		expect	use
		need	

Verbs That *Must* Be Followed by a Noun or Pronoun Object Before an Infinitive

A noun or pronoun object *must* follow these verbs if an infinitive is used. The object comes between the verb and the infinitive. Note that *for* is not used before the noun or pronoun.

Verb + noun or pronoun + infinitive	The doctor **encouraged him to get** more exercise.	advise*	order
	She **persuaded him to start** a regular exercise program.	allow*	permit*
		cause*	persuade
		convince	remind
		encourage*	require
		force	teach*
		get	tell
		hire	urge
		invite	warn

■ **EXERCISE C** Complete the following sentences by using *for*, or use *X* to indicate that nothing is needed.

Example   We asked *X*   Mary to go camping with us.

It was difficult *for* her to decide.

1. We had expected _____ her to say yes immediately.

2. She promised _____ us to ask for vacation time.

3. It wasn't easy _____ her to get time off from work.

---

* These verbs are followed by gerunds if no (pro)noun object is used after the main verb. See Part Four for more information.

4. We told _____ her to keep trying.

5. We finally convinced _____ Mary to come.

6. Then she invited _____ her friend to come.

7. In order _____ both of them to come, we had to find a bigger tent.

8. Our neighbor wanted _____ us to use his tent.

■ **EXERCISE D** Complete the following passage by using active or passive infinitive or gerund forms of the verbs in parentheses. Be sure to include negatives or noun objects when indicated.

BICYCLING

1. Bicycles were invented in the early nineteenth century as "toys" for the rich, the only people who could afford _to buy_____ (buy) the early models. Later, bikes became more affordable, but few people would dare _____ (risk) _____ (fall) in order _____ (try) one.

2. By 1899, one out of every six Americans had managed _____ _____ (buy) a bike and _____ (learn) how _____ (ride) it. The bicycle boom was on! Even the *New York Times* hired _____ (reporters / cover) races and encouraged _____ (local groups / sponsor) bicycling events. But then the automobile was invented, and its popularity threatened _____ (eliminate) the bicycle entirely.

3. The 1970s and the oil crisis brought new popularity to the bicycle when the government urged _____ (Americans / drive / not) as much. At the same time, doctors were advising _____ (people / get) more exercise. Bicycle sales climbed from fewer than seven million in 1970 to over fifteen million in 1973.

4. The popularity of _____ (bicycle) is expected

_____ (keep) _____ (in-

crease) as millions of people worldwide rely on bikes for transporta-

tion and recreation. In fact, in Washington, D.C., alone, over seventy

thousand bicyclists commute to their jobs daily. These cyclists risk

_____ (hit) by cars, and they have _____

_____ (tolerate) _____ (breathe) exhaust-

filled air. Yet bicycle commuters have learned _____

_____ (live) with these hazards. They refuse _____

_____ (give up) the exercise and the low cost of

_____ (ride) a bicycle to work every day.

■ **EXERCISE E** Complete the following passage with gerund or infinitive forms of the verbs in parentheses. Include negatives and objects
where indicated.

THE SIMPLE LIFE: CAMPING

Camping _____ (camp) can teach you many things, such as how

_____ ₁ (recognize) plants and animals, _____

_____ ₂ (set up) a tent, and _____ ₃ (read) a

map. Most of all, you can anticipate _____ ₄ (under-

stand) more about yourself and your place in nature.

Whether you decide _____ ₅ (hike) into the wil-

derness, _____ ₆ (travel) by canoe, or simply

_____ ₇ (drive) to a nearby campground, you are

probably looking for some of the same experiences. Most campers

hope _____ ₈ (find) a simpler lifestyle. They tend

_____ ₉ (forget) about work and worries while they

enjoy _____ ₁₀ (be) outdoors.

Because the number of U.S. campers is increasing daily, the National

Park Service advises _____ ₁₁ (outdoor lovers /

remember) several things. First, although it encourages _____

_____₁₂ (campers / enjoy) the outdoors, it urges _____

_____₁₃ (everyone / treat) nature with respect. That involves

_____₁₄ (leave) your campsite *cleaner* than you

found it. It involves _____₁₅ (learn) _____

_____₁₆ (enjoy) the natural world of plants and animals without

_____₁₇ (disturb) it. Remember that wild animals *are*

wild, and they can hurt you, just as you can hurt them.

The park service invites _____₁₈ (you / enjoy) and

_____₁₉ (explore) the world of nature, but at the same

time, it expects _____₂₀ (you / protect) each area

you visit so that future generations may look forward to

_____₂₁ (have) similar enjoyable experiences.

P A R T   F O U R

Verbs Followed by Either Gerunds or Infinitives

GAMES PEOPLE PLAY

Some people love to compete on the tennis court, and others like to compete on the chessboard. Me, I've always preferred playing Monopoly. I remember playing all night quite often, and sometimes I would continue playing into the morning. I just couldn't stop building those hotels!

VERBS FOLLOWED BY EITHER GERUNDS OR INFINITIVES

These verbs may be followed by either gerunds or infinitives without affecting the basic meaning of the sentence.

Verb + gerund	It **began raining.**	begin	love*
Verb + infinitive	It **began to rain.**	can't stand	neglect
		continue	prefer
		hate	start
		like*	

VERBS FOLLOWED BY GERUNDS OR INFINITIVES, DEPENDING ON THE USE OF A NOUN OR PRONOUN OBJECT

These verbs are followed by gerunds if no noun or pronoun object is used. If a noun or pronoun object is used, they must be followed by infinitives.

Verb + gerund	We **don't permit smoking** here.	advise	encourage
		allow	permit
Verb + noun or pronoun + infinitive	They **permitted him to smoke** in the other room.	cause	teach

■ **EXERCISE A**   Complete the following conversation by using gerund or infinitive forms of the verbs in parentheses. Note any instance where either an infinitive or a gerund is possible.

HELEN: Harry, let's play some tennis today. You know I love

to play (playing) (play) tennis on a nice day.

HARRY: I would love _____₁ (play) a set or two,

but my elbow hurts. I've decided _____₂

(play / not) tennis until it feels better.

HELEN: But Harry, you haven't played tennis in months!

HARRY: Oh yes, I have. I played a set with you in December.

HELEN: That was five months ago. Well, then, would you like

_____₃ (go) roller-skating?

---

* Remember that *would like* and *would love* are followed by infinitives. See Part Two.

HARRY: You know that I really like _____4 (roller-skate), but my knee hurts.

HELEN: Harry, I'm going to get upset if you continue _____5 (make) excuses. You're just plain lazy!

HARRY: No, I'm not. Besides, there's a golf tournament on TV today.

HELEN: Harry, I can't stand _____6 (see) any more boring TV shows. Let's *do* something.

■ **EXERCISE B** Complete the following conversation by using gerund or infinitive forms of the verbs in parentheses. Add noun or pronoun objects when indicated, paying careful attention to the use of gerunds and infinitives. Note where either an infinitive or a gerund is possible.

DOCTOR: What happened, Harry?

HARRY: Well, Doctor, my knee suddenly began

to hurt (hurting) (hurt) several weeks ago, but I've neglected _____1 (do) anything about it until now. I prefer _____2 (go / not) to a doctor unless it's absolutely necessary.

HELEN: He may not like _____3 (go) to the doctor, but he certainly loves _____4 (complain) about his aches and pains!

DOCTOR: I don't find anything obviously wrong, Harry. But I'd advise _____5 (you / take) it easy for a week. I'd advise _____6 (do / not) heavy exercise.

HELEN: Doctor, please don't encourage _____7 (Harry / be) lazy. If he continues _____8 (sit) at home, he'll get even lazier. I just can't stand _____9 (watch) another day of television. It's already started _____10 (drive) me crazy!

DOCTOR: I said *heavy* exercise. That allows _____11 (Harry / do) other activities. I encourage _____12 (he / do) any form of moderate exercise.

Verbs That Change Meaning Depending on the Use of Infinitives or Gerunds

These verbs may be followed by either infinitives or gerunds, but the choice between infinitives and gerunds affects the meaning of the sentence.

	EXAMPLES	MEANINGS
mean + infinitive	I **meant to visit** Brazil.	I planned to visit Brazil, but I couldn't.
mean + gerund	A trip to Brazil **meant spending** much more money. It **meant spending** much more money.	A trip to Brazil involved spending much more money.
remember + infinitive	I always **remember to buy** the paper.	I never forget to buy the paper.
remember + gerund	I **remember buying** the paper.	I remember that I bought the paper.
stop, quit + infinitive	He **stopped (quit) to smoke.**	He stopped his work in order to smoke a cigarette.
stop, quit + gerund	He **stopped (quit) smoking.**	He does not smoke anymore.
try + infinitive	The room was hot, so we **tried to open** the window.	We were not able to open the window.
try + gerund	The room was hot, so we tried the fan, but it didn't work. Then we **tried opening** the window.	The window was another possibility.

■ **EXERCISE C** Complete the following by using the infinitive or the gerund forms of the verbs in parentheses.

1. After the volleyball game, we all stopped <u>*to have*</u> (have) a cup of coffee, but Joanie didn't join us. She said that she had stopped _____ (drink) coffee because the caffeine bothered her.

2. Everyone at work was surprised when John quit _____ (take) a long vacation in South America. He said that we should quit _____ (be) so responsible and take off for faraway places too!

3. "I tried _____ (open) the front door, but it's stuck."

   "Have you tried _____ (use) the key? It's locked, you know."

4. "Did you remember _____ (buy) a Monopoly game?"

   "Of course, I didn't remember _____ (buy) one. I didn't know that you wanted one."

   "You knew, but you forgot _____ (get) one. I distinctly remember _____ (tell) you _____ (buy) one this morning. This means _____ (postpone) our party tonight."

   "You meant _____ (tell) me, but *you* forgot. I didn't forget!"

■ **EXERCISE D   Review of Infinitives and Gerunds**   Complete the following passage by using infinitive or gerund forms of the verbs in parentheses.

MONOPOLY

Monopoly, Parker Brothers' game of *buying*_____ (buy) and _____₁ (sell) real estate, was invented in 1933 by an unemployed engineer, Charles Darrow. Darrow had lost his job at the beginning of the Depression, and although he had continued

_____₂ (look) everywhere, he hadn't been able _____₃ (find) steady work in three years. During those years, he tried _____₄ (walk) dogs and _____₅ (fix) electric irons _____₆ (make) some money. _____₇ (keep) busy, he invented things.

First, Darrow tried _____₈ (create) puzzles, but no one was interested in _____₉ (buy) his ideas. Finally, he began _____₁₀ (dream) about the days before the Depression, when he and his wife had been able _____₁₁ (afford) _____₁₂ (take) vacations. He remembered _____₁₃ (visit) Atlantic City, New Jersey, and he started _____₁₄ (draw) maps of the streets. From these, he developed his game.

The Darrows began _____₁₅ (spend) every evening _____₁₆ (buy), _____₁₇ (rent), _____₁₈ (develop), and _____₁₉ (sell) "real estate." There was no television in those days, and they couldn't afford _____₂₀ (go) to the movies. _____₂₁ (play) with large amounts of money and property was entertaining, however, even if neither was real. Soon friends began _____₂₂ (stop by) in the evenings _____₂₃ (try) _____₂₄ (play) the game.

Darrow's friends and neighbors asked _____₂₅ (he / make) sets for them. After a while, Darrow could not make enough sets _____₂₆ (satisfy) the demand for them, so he went to Parker Brothers with his game. At first, Parker Brothers rejected it, but that didn't discourage Darrow from _____₂₇ (try) again. Soon Parker Brothers made him an offer.

Today Monopoly is the most popular game in the world. It is sold in fifteen languages.

Causative Verbs and Related Structures; Verbs of Perception; Present and Past Participles Used as Adjectives

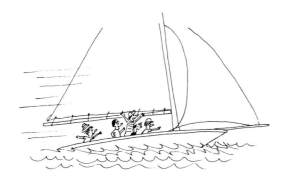

SAILING

Nothing is more thrilling than sailing over white-capped waves on a bright blue day. You feel the sun burning your cheeks, and you see the seagulls diving for fish. You get excited! It makes you feel alive.

CAUSATIVE VERBS AND RELATED STRUCTURES

Help, Let, and *Make*

These verbs are followed by the simple form of a second verb. They are not generally followed by passive constructions. Note that the use of *to* after *help* is optional.

help	I **helped** (him) **carry** the packages. I **helped** (him) **to carry** the packages.	*Help* may take the simple form or the infinitive of another verb as an object.
let	I **let** him **borrow** my car. I **let** them **help** me.	*Let* is followed by a noun or pronoun and the simple form of another verb. It does *not* take an infinitive.
make	I **made** him **wash** my car. I **made** them **help** me. The news **made** me **unhappy**. The bad weather **made** us **late**.	*Make* is followed by a noun or pronoun and the simple form of another verb. *Make* + noun or pronoun + adjective is also frequently used.

$\longrightarrow$

Have, Get, and *Need*

These verbs are often followed by the active or passive form of a second verb.

have	**ACTIVE** I **had** him **wash** my car. I **had** the barber **cut** my hair. **PASSIVE** I **had** my car **washed** (by him). I **had** my hair **cut** (by the barber).	Constructions with *have* are often used when you pay for a service. You *have* someone *do* something, or you *have* something *done* by someone.
get **need**	**ACTIVE** I **got** him **to wash** my car. I **needed** him **to wash** my car. **PASSIVE** I **got** my car **washed** (by him). I **needed** my car **washed** (by him).	The passive construction of *get* is similar in meaning to the passive construction of *have. Get* is frequently used in conversational English.

■ **EXERCISE A** Traveling is fun, but both travel and transportation can cause many problems. Imagine that you've been on a long trip and you're telling about a few of the difficulties you had. Use the following cues to form complete sentences.

Example   the boat ride / feel seasick
The boat ride made me feel seasick.

1. the plane ride / become airsick
2. the bus ride through the mountains / feel dizzy
3. the food / get sick
4. the taxi drivers / fear for my life
5. the traffic / arrive late everywhere

■ **YOUR TURN** Think about the last trip you took. What were some of your reactions to the sights, sounds, smells, food, and weather? Add at least four sentences using your own ideas with *make.*

■ **EXERCISE B** Answer the following questions in complete sentences.

1. In general, do you let other people borrow things from you?
2. Would you let your best friend use something you really value?
3. If it were lost or stolen, would you make your best friend replace it?
4. If it were damaged, would you have your friend pay for repairs?

■ **EXERCISE C** Imagine you are planning to take a trip. Think of all the preparations you will need to make before you leave. Complete the following sentences with appropriate past participles.

Example   I'll have an itinerary *planned* _____ by a travel
agent.

1. I'll have reservations _____ at a hotel.
2. I'll get my car _____ .
3. I'll need the mail _____ at the post office.
4. I'll need my plants _____ .
5. I'll have my clothes _____ at the cleaners.
6. I'll get my suitcases _____ .

■ **EXERCISE D** When you have your car checked before a long trip, what do you have done? Use the following cues to form complete sentences with *have, need,* or *get*.

Example   car / wash
         I get (have) the car washed.

1. the oil / change   4. the spare tire / repair
2. the brakes / adjust   5. the engine / tune
3. the tires / check

■ **YOUR TURN** What are some repairs or services that you've had done lately? Try to list at least four.

Example   I had (got) my last roll of film developed.

_____
_____
_____
_____

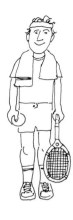

■ **EXERCISE E** Complete the following passage with appropriate forms of the verbs in parentheses.

BJORN: Jack, this is Bjorn. I'm taking a little trip, and I need a few things. Have someone *buy* (buy) me some tennis balls. Oh, and get someone _____₁ (make) two reservations on the next flight to Rio de Janeiro.

JACK: Anything else you want?

BJORN: Yes, get my white suit _____₂ (press) and my white hat _____₃ (clean). Have my bags _____₄ (pack) and ready to go in an hour. Oh, and I need a letter _____₅ (send) to my attorney. Tell her to have a contract _____₆ (write) for those new TV commercials. I'll let you _____₇ (take) care of the details.

JACK: All right. Have a nice time. When are you coming back?

BJORN: Sunday! Have someone _____₈ (meet) me at the airport.

VERBS OF PERCEPTION

The verbs *see, look (at), watch, observe, listen (to), hear, smell, taste, perceive,* and *feel* can be followed by a second verb. The second verb can be in the simple or the present participle form. Often there is no great difference in meaning between the two forms, however.

Present participle	We **heard** the bell **ringing.**	action in progress
Simple form	We **heard** the bell **ring.**	action probably completed
Present participle	We **saw** the building **burning** down.	action in progress
Simple form	We **saw** the building **burn** down.	action probably completed

■ **EXERCISE F** Imagine that you have just taken a boat ride. Use the information in parentheses to complete the following sentences describing what you saw, heard, felt, and so on.

Example We saw (seagulls / fly around the boat).
We saw seagulls flying around the boat.
We saw seagulls fly around the boat.

1. We watched (birds / dive for fish).
2. We heard (waves / crash into the boat).
3. We felt (saltwater / burn our cheeks).
4. We watched (sail / fill with air).
5. We felt (wind / blow across our faces).
6. We saw (ocean / become stormy).

PRESENT AND PAST PARTICIPLES USED AS ADJECTIVES

The participle forms of many verbs may also be used as adjectives after verbs such as *be, become, feel,* and *get*. Verbs that express emotions are often used in this way.

Verb	The ideas in that book **interested** me. The plot **fascinated** me.	Verbs that are often used in this way include *amaze, annoy, astonish, bore, confuse, disappoint, excite, fascinate, frighten, inspire, interest, please, relax, satisfy, surprise, thrill, tire,* and *worry.*
Present participle	The ideas in that book were very **interesting** (to me).	The present participle shows an effect on someone or something.
Past participle	I was very **interested in** the ideas in that book. I get more **excited about** the subject every day. I don't feel **bored with** that book.	The past participle shows a reaction to someone or something. A variety of prepositions are used with the past participle.

■ **EXERCISE G** Think about a movie or TV program that you've seen recently. Give a short review of the movie by answering the following questions.

1. Why were you interested in seeing the movie?
2. Was the plot interesting?
3. Were you surprised by the ending?
4. Was the language confusing?
5. Did you ever get bored during the movie?
6. Were you tired by the end of the movie, or were you relaxed (excited, fascinated, etc.)?

■ **YOUR TURN** Think about a trip you've taken; a sport you've played; or a restaurant, store, or museum you've visited during the past few weeks. Give several original sentences using either present or past participles. Choose from the following verbs or add your own.

POSITIVE FEELINGS		NEGATIVE FEELINGS	
amaze	interest	annoy	disappoint
amuse	intrigue	bewilder	shock
excite	relax	bore	tire
fascinate	surprise	confuse	worry

■ **EXERCISE H** Complete the following by using either the present or the past participle of the verbs in parentheses.

Example   Staying underwater is _frightening_____ (frighten) to many people.

1. Some people get _____ (worry) about staying underwater for a long time.

2. Yet people everywhere are _____ (interest) in trying scuba diving.

3. Scuba diving is _____ (excite) to many people.

4. They are _____ (thrill) about seeing exotic fish and coral.

5. It is _____ (amaze) to see the variety of fish and plant life that exists underwater.

6. Divers are _____ (surprise / often) by the friendliness of some of the sea animals and fish.

■ **EXERCISE I Review** Complete the
following passage by using appropriate
forms (simple, infinitive, gerund, or present
or past participle) of the verbs in parentheses. In some cases, more than one form is
correct. Try to give all possibilities.

RIDE THE WIND

_____₁ (windsurf) is the "hottest," coolest, smoothest, and fastest way _____₂ (sail) across the water.
"It's _____₃ (thrill)," says one windsurfer. "When I
catch the wind, I let myself _____₄ (go), and soon I
feel myself _____₅ (fly) across the water! It makes me
_____₆ (want) _____₇ (keep) on
_____₈ (go) without ever _____₉
(stop). I get so _____₁₀ (excite) that I forget how far
from shore I've gone."

_____₁₁ (windsurf) is the sport for water lovers
who want _____₁₂ (have) a great time even though
they aren't able _____₁₃ (get) to the ocean regularly.
You can try the sport on a lake or even a pond. If you decide
_____₁₄ (try) it, remember one thing: _____
_____₁₅ (learn) _____₁₆ (windsurf) usually
means a lot of falls into the water. Plan _____₁₇ (get)
very wet your first day. But after one day of _____₁₈
(fall), you can expect _____₁₉ (master) the art.
_____₂₀ (windsurf) is all a matter of
_____₂₁ (practice) balance and position, and you can
usually have someone _____₂₂ (teach) you in three to

six hours. Soon you will begin _____ ₂₃ (feel) your

body _____ ₂₄ (move) with the board. Most wind-

surfers seem _____ ₂₅ (agree) that if you know how

_____ ₂₆ (ride) a bike, you can learn _____

_____ ₂₇ (windsurf). Just remember _____ ₂₈

(pick) a hot day or _____ ₂₉ (rent) a wetsuit because

there is no way _____ ₃₀ (avoid) _____

_____ ₃₁ (get) wet.

PART SIX

Language Activities

These speaking and writing activities are designed to help you practice the
variety of verb forms covered in this chapter — gerund, infinitive, present
and past participles, and simple form.

GERUNDS WITH ADJECTIVE-PREPOSITION COMBINATIONS

■ **ACTIVITY A**   In pairs or small groups, use the following phrases in a
discussion of your favorite pastimes (sports, hobbies, arts, crafts). After
you have finished, choose one member of your group to give a brief summary of your discussion for the entire class.

I'm interested in . . .	It's fun . . .
I'm excited about . . .	It's enjoyable . . .
I'm afraid of . . .	It's boring . . .
I'm good at . . .	It's interesting . . .

Example   **I'm interested in photography. I'm not very good at
using all the different lenses, but it's fun. For me, it's
always enjoyable to take pictures and develop my own
film. And it's less expensive for me to do it myself.**

GERUNDS VERSUS INFINITIVES

■ **ACTIVITY B** Have you ever visited an astrologer or a fortune-teller? In many cultures, telling the future is an important art. Some people tell the future through the stars; others tell it through tea leaves, coffee grounds, or crystal balls. Today use your grammar book to tell the future. Work in pairs or in small groups and role-play a visit to a fortune-teller. Use the following with gerunds or infinitives in your role-plays.

Example Do you really want . . . ?
Do you really want to know your future?

1. It will involve . . .
2. You seem . . .
3. Your future appears . . .
4. I can't help . . .
5. You can anticipate . . .
6. You had better (not) hope . . .
7. Have you considered . . . ?
8. You must learn . . .
9. You need . . .
10. I suggest . . .

■ **ACTIVITY C** In small groups, make up a story together. One member of your group will begin with a sentence, and the rest will add to it to create an entire story. Each student must talk continuously for at least thirty seconds. As you tell the story, keep your book open to pages 264–267 and use as many of the verbs on the lists as possible. (To make this activity more difficult, you may use the rule that no verb can be repeated!) Try to use an infinitive or gerund with each. You may use your own opening to begin the story, or you may use one of the following lines.

1. "It was a dark and stormy night."
2. "Romeo, Romeo, wherefore art thou Romeo?"
3. "As Gregor Samsa awoke one morning from uneasy dreams, he found himself transformed in his bed into a gigantic insect."
4. "Once upon a time there lived . . . "
5. "This is the tale of a meeting of two lonesome, skinny, fairly old men on a planet which was dying fast . . . "

VERBS OF PERCEPTION

■ **ACTIVITY D** Traveling to faraway places is one of the most fascinating ways to spend your leisure time. Imagine yourself in the Middle East, the Amazon, or Paris. Imagine where you have been and how you arrived at this destination. Imagine what you will do next. As you imagine, describe everything you see, hear, smell, feel, and perceive. Are you excited? Are you nervous? What are the most interesting things around you?

Creativity

Adverb Clauses

In this chapter, you will review the variety of sentence types in English, and you will begin to study complex sentences. You will focus on complex sentences with adverb clauses. As you study the chapter, note the relationships between ideas and the variety of ways these relationships can be expressed. Also pay attention to the punctuation used with each type of clause.

Previewing the Passage

Creativity is a difficult concept to define because it means different things to different people. What does creativity mean to you?

The Creative Urge

If an inventor builds an amazing machine or an artist produces a magnificent piece of artwork, we call this creative process genius. Creativity is not only in the realm of artists and scientists, however. It is an attribute we all have within us. The creative urge is the most deeply human — and the most mysterious —
5   of all our attributes. Although we don't completely understand how or why, each of us is creative.

Since our history began, we humans have produced marvelous inventions. Learning to use fire and to make tools were incredibly creative achievements. Above all, early humans produced our most extraordinary creation —
10   language.

After our ancestors had learned to communicate with one another, a long series of amazing developments began. Creativity flourished among such peoples as the ancient Egyptians, Greeks, and Mayans. Long before the modern age of machines, our ancestors had already developed sophisticated tech-
15   niques and systems in mathematics, astronomy, engineering, art, architecture, and literature.

Of course, some societies had more achievements than others. For example, while the Egyptians were developing mathematics and building libraries, other societies were still learning to use fire. By the time Europe began to use
20   money, China had already traded with paper currency for hundreds of years. Nevertheless, every new accomplishment represents human creativity — whether it is due to fulfillment of a need or to pure curiosity. If one attribute characterizes humans, it is our creative urge to improve our lives, to find new and better ways of doing things.

Understanding Vocabulary

1. *To create* means "to bring into being, to cause to exist." Other forms of *create* are *creation* (*n.*), *creator* (*n.*), *creativity* (*n.*), *creative* (*adj.*), and *creatively* (*adv.*). Complete these sentences with the correct form of *create*.

    a. Dora designs clothes. She is a very *creative* _____
        designer.

    b. She tries _____ attractive and unusual designs.

    c. Dora has been working _____ in art and
       clothing design for many years.

    d. Her _____ have become so popular that she
       has recently opened her own boutique.

    e. Everyone admires Dora's _____ .

    f. She is a _____ of new styles and trends in
      fashion.

2. Many verbs add *-er* to describe a person who does that action. For
   example, a person who works is a *worker*. Other verbs use the *-or*
   ending, however. For example, a person who creates is called a *creator*. Give the spelling of the noun form of each of these verbs.
   a. act
   b. govern
   c. inspect
   d. invent
   e. visit

3. Match the synonyms. In some cases, more than one synonym is
   possible.

societies	accomplishments
marvelous	amazing
magnificent	attributes
extraordinary	develop
currency	invention
create	money
creation	peoples
characteristics	
achievements	

Discussing Ideas

1. What are some activities that you consider creative? Who are some
   people that you consider creative? Why?
2. What has your culture created that is unusual or unique?
3. Imagine that you have the ability to create anything you want. What
   would you like to create?

PART ONE

Sentence Types, Coordinating Conjunctions, and Clauses of Time and Condition—Present and Future Time

WHAT IS CREATIVITY?

To create means "to bring into being, to cause to exist." According to this dictionary definition, ordinary people are creative every day. We are creative whenever we look at or think about something in a new way.

SENTENCE TYPES

Sentences may be simple, compound, complex, or a combination of compound and complex.

Simple	Creativity is part of everyday life.	Simple sentences have one subject/verb combination.
Compound	Many artists are highly creative, **but** ordinary people can be just as creative.	Compound sentences are two simple sentences connected by *and, but, for, nor, or, so,* or *yet.*
	Some people are creative from childhood; **however,** others show their genius later in life.	A compound sentence may also be formed by joining two sentences with a semicolon. Transition words or phrases are often used with compound sentences.

→

Complex	**Although** some people are creative from childhood, others show their genius later in life.	Complex sentences consist of two or more clauses: a main clause that is complete by itself and one or more dependent clauses introduced by a connecting word such as *although, because, if, that, when, while,* or *who.*

■ **EXERCISE A Sentence Types** Label subjects(s) and verb(s) in the following sentences. Then indicate what type of sentence each is (simple, compound, or complex). If the sentence is compound or complex, circle the connecting word. Underline the *dependent* clauses in complex sentences.

Example   We are creative whenever we look at or think about something in a new way.   *Complex*

1. First of all, creativity involves an awareness of our surroundings.

2. It is the ability to notice things that others might miss.

3. A second part of creativity is an ability to see relationships among things.

4. Creativity is involved when we remake or reorganize the old in new ways.

5. We might find a more efficient way to study, or we could rearrange our furniture in a better way.

6. Third, creativity means having the courage and drive to make use of our new ideas.

7. To think up a new concept is one thing; to put the idea to work is another.

8. These three aspects of creativity are involved in all the great works of genius; however, they are also involved in many of our day-to-day activities.

■ **EXERCISE B** **Compound Sentences**   Form compound sentences using the coordinating conjunction(s) indicated for each set. Change word or sentence order when necessary. Also change nouns to pronouns and add commas. For sentences with more than one possibility, form two sentences and try to explain any difference in meaning or in emphasis.

Example   (nor) Some people do not use all of their senses very often. They do not have a very great awareness of their surroundings.
Some people do not use their senses very often, nor do they have a very great awareness of their surroundings.

1. (but / yet)   Some people use all five senses often.
Most of us rely heavily on our sight.
2. (nor)   Many people do not pay attention to sounds.
Many people do not take time to listen.
3. (for / so)   Musicians pay attention to all types of sounds.
Musicians want to find interesting new combinations.
4. (and / yet)   A musician can find music in exotic sounds.
A musician may also hear music in ordinary noises.
5. (or / and)   A car horn may produce a new rhythm.
A bird may sing a new sequence of notes.
6. (but / yet)   Another person may not hear these combinations.
A music lover will find these combinations.

ADVERB CLAUSES OF TIME — UNSPECIFIED OR PRESENT TIME

Time clauses can relate ideas or actions that occur at the same time or in a sequence. These may be habitual, repeated activities, or they may be occurring in the present. Note that these clauses may begin or end sentences.

HABITUAL ACTIVITIES

when	**When** Tim Astor gets a new idea for a novel, he writes it down immediately.	*When* joins two actions that happen at the same time or that happen one immediately after the other. In many cases, *when* means "at any time" and is the equivalent of *whenever*. The simple present is generally used in both clauses.
whenever	He begins a new book **whenever** he gets an inspiration.	

$\longrightarrow$

HABITUAL ACTIVITIES

after	He edits his material **after** he finishes the entire first draft.	*After, before,* and *until* join actions that occur in sequence. Either the simple present or the present perfect may be used in the dependent clause. The present perfect emphasizes the completion of the action.
before	He never starts a new project **before** he has completed the current one.	
until	He works on a project **until** he is fully satisfied with it.	
as	**As** he is writing, he often listens to classical music.	*As* and *while* may join two actions that happen at about the same time. The present continuous can be used in the dependent clause to emphasize the continuous nature of the activity. The verb in the main clause determines whether the action is habitual or happening at the moment of speaking.
while	He often listens to music **while** he is writing.	

PRESENT ACTIVITIES

as	Tonight he is listening to Beethoven's Fifth Symphony **as** he is writing.	*As* and *while* can also join two actions that are happening at the present. In this case, both clauses are in the present continuous.
while	He is humming **while** he is writing.	

PAST AND PRESENT ACTIVITIES

since	He has been writing **since** he woke up at six this morning.	*Since* joins a previous action or situation to an action or situation in progress. The main clause is in the present perfect (continuous).

■ **EXERCISE C** Complete the following with present forms of the verbs in parentheses.

A METHOD TO OUR MADNESS

For most of us, when we _think_____ (think) of the work of creative artists and scientists, we _____₁ (imagine) a mysterious world of geniuses. When an inventor _____₂ (develop) an amazing new machine, when a musician _____₃ (create) a beautiful piece of music, or when a scientist _____₄ (make) a major discovery, we _____₅ (feel) in awe. We _____₆ (assume) that these geniuses _____₇ (be) very different from us. Yet, geniuses or not, we all _____₈ (use) a similar creative process whenever we _____₉ (look) at something in a new way or _____₁₀ (try) new solutions to a problem. It _____₁₁ (be) a process of first looking at a situation carefully and then making and following a plan of action.

■ **EXERCISE D** Think about the process of writing a composition. Make a step-by-step plan of action for writing by forming complete sentences from the clauses below. Try to give at least two completions for each step. You may want to add more steps.

Example Whenever you write something,
you have to concentrate on your ideas.
you should find a quiet place without distractions.

1. Before you begin to write a composition, . . .
2. While you are thinking about the topic, . . .
3. After you have gathered your ideas, . . .
4. When you need more information on a topic, . . .
5. . . . as you are writing.
6. After you have finished writing, . . .
7. . . . until you are satisfied with your composition.
8. . . . before you hand in your composition.

■ **EXERCISE E** Describe the following process by making statements with time clauses. Add modal auxiliaries such as *can* or *should* and combine steps when necessary. Explain what you should do before you begin the process, what you should do while you are completing the process, and what you should do after you have finished.

Example   **Before you begin painting, you should choose a good piece of watercolor paper. After you have sketched your drawing lightly, . . .**

Painting a watercolor

- Choose a good piece of watercolor paper.
- Sketch your drawing lightly.
- Wet the paper with water.
- Use watery paint for large areas.
- Catch any drips.
- Use a drier brush for details.
- Let your painting dry completely.
- Mount your picture.

■ **YOUR TURN** Give a brief description of another process that you are familiar with. It may be part of a hobby or craft, or it may be some other process.

FACTUAL CONDITIONAL SENTENCES — UNSPECIFIED OR PRESENT TIME

if	**If** Tim writes a lot during the week, he usually has time to relax on the weekend. Tim usually has time to relax on the weekend **if** he writes a lot during the week.	The main clause is the effect or result of the dependent clause. These sentences refer to habitual activities or activities that are true in general.
unless	Tim rarely writes on the week-end **unless** he has a deadline. **Unless** he has a deadline, Tim doesn't work on the weekend.	*Unless* is used similarly to *if . . . not* in many sentences. However, *unless* is more emphatic.

■ **EXERCISE F** According to Paul Heist in *The Creative College Student*, these are some of the chief characteristics of creative students and creative people in general: *Creative people are flexible, independent, innovative, spontaneous, and open to a wide range of experiences. They develop their own styles and their own sense of beauty.*

The following deals with some of these characteristics. Form complete sentences from each pair by matching a main clause with a dependent clause. Pay attention to the difference in meaning of *if* and *unless*.

Example   If you develop your own style, . . . *b*
              Unless you develop your own style, . . . *a*
              a. you end up imitating other people.
              b. you don't have to imitate other people.

1. If a person is independent, . . .
   Unless a person is independent, . . .
   a. he or she usually relies on others for support or encouragement.
   b. he or she doesn't have to depend on others for support or encouragement.
2. If you are flexible, . . .
   Unless you are flexible, . . .
   a. you can adapt more easily to new situations.
   b. it may be difficult for you to adapt to new situations.
3. If people are open to new ideas, . . .
   Unless people are open to new ideas, . . .
   a. they can take better advantage of unusual opportunities.
   b. they may miss many unusual opportunities.
4. If you are innovative, . . .
   Unless you are innovative, . . .
   a. it may be difficult for you to find solutions for many problems.
   b. you can usually find solutions for most problems.

FACTUAL CONDITIONAL SENTENCES — FUTURE TIME

Factual conditional sentences that refer to the future generally express predictions or intentions. The main clause shows the effect or result of the dependent clause.

if	**If** Tim finishes his newest novel this week, it will be published in about six months. The novel is going to go on sale in December **if** he can finish it this week.	The verb in the dependent clause is in a present tense. The verb in the main clause is *be going to* or a modal auxiliary: *will, may, might, should,* etc.

$\longrightarrow$

unless	**Unless** Tim finishes this week, the book won't go on sale until next January.	*Unless* is similar in meaning to *if . . . not* in many sentences, but *unless* is more emphatic.

■ **EXERCISE G** Imagine that you are trying to decide about places to live. Use the following decision tree to help you decide what to do. Use the correct forms of the verbs in parentheses and add more information. Then make your decision and explain why you made that decision.

I can spend up to $500 a month for my expenses (housing, meals, and transportation).

Apartment A: with Americans; $280 a month; near school
Apartment B: with people from my own country; $200 a month; far from school

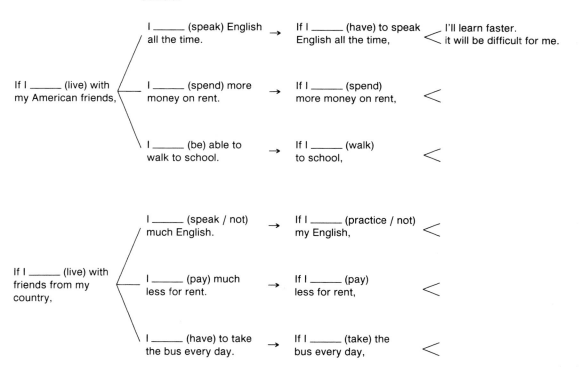

■ **YOUR TURN** Think of a decision that you must make soon. Then make a decision tree. Think of all the effects of each action and write them on your decision tree. Use this information to help you make your decision.

■ **EXERCISE H** Combine the following pairs to form new sentences with *unless*.

Example   I should speak English more often. If I don't, I'll never become fluent.
Unless I speak English more often, I'll never become fluent.

1. I should find a cheaper place to live. If I don't, I'll run out of money soon.
2. We should save more money. If we don't, we'll never be able to take a long vacation.
3. You should send your application for school soon. If you don't, you may not be accepted this year.
4. I should write my parents soon. If I don't, they'll start to get worried about me.
5. You should start your research project soon. If you don't, you may not be able to finish in time.

PART TWO

Comparisons

A PICTURE IS WORTH A THOUSAND WORDS

Without ever saying a word, Charlie Chaplin has made more people laugh than perhaps any other comic artist. Chaplin has been called "the most universal human being of our time."

COMPARISONS WITH ADJECTIVES AND ADVERBS

The positive forms of adjectives and adverbs are used in expressions with (*not*) *as . . . as* (*as slow as, not as slow as*). Comparative forms are used to compare two things. Superlative forms are used to discuss three or more things. *The* is generally used with superlative forms. (See pages 254 and 255 for spelling guidelines.)

	POSITIVE	COMPARATIVE	SUPERLATIVE

Add *-er* and *-est* to the following.

	POSITIVE	COMPARATIVE	SUPERLATIVE
One-syllable adjectives	nice	nicer	the nicest
	young	younger	the youngest
Adjectives and adverbs that have the same form	early	earlier	the earliest
	fast	faster	the fastest
	hard	harder	the hardest
	late	later	the latest

Add *-er* and *-est* or use *more, less, the most,* and *the least* with the following.

	POSITIVE	COMPARATIVE	SUPERLATIVE
Most two-syllable adjectives	clever	cleverer	the cleverest
		more clever	the most clever
	funny	funnier	the funniest*
		more funny	the most funny
	simple	simpler	the simplest*
		more simple	the most simple

Use *more, less, the most,* or *the least* with the following.

	POSITIVE	COMPARATIVE	SUPERLATIVE
Two-syllable adjectives that end in *-ed, -ful, -ing, -ish, -ous, -st,* and *-x*	complex	more complex	the most complex
	famous	more famous	the most famous
	interesting	more interesting	the most interesting
	worried	more worried	the most worried

Use *more, less, the most,* or *the least* with the following.

	POSITIVE	COMPARATIVE	SUPERLATIVE
Longer adjectives and most *-ly* adverbs	difficult	more difficult	the most difficult
	quickly	more quickly	the most quickly

$\longrightarrow$

---

*With words ending in *-y* and *-le,* the *-er* and *-est* forms are more common.

Irregular Adjectives and Adverbs

ADJECTIVE	ADVERB	COMPARATIVE	SUPERLATIVE
bad	badly	worse	(the) worst
good	—	better	(the) best
well	well	better	(the) best
far	far	farther	(the) farthest (distance)
		further	(the) furthest
little	little	less	(the) least
many	—	more	(the) most
much	much	more	(the) most

■ **EXERCISE A Oral Practice** Give the comparative and superlative forms of each of the following words.

Examples   hot   **hotter**   **the hottest**
             quickly   **more quickly**   **the most quickly**

1. easy
2. difficult
3. fast
4. slowly
5. pretty
6. handsome
7. interesting
8. sad
9. bad
10. far
11. hard
12. worried

■ **EXERCISE B** Complete the following with comparative or superlative forms of the adjectives in parentheses. Add *the* when necessary.

1. Born in 1889 in England, (Sir) Charlie Chaplin was widely rated as

   _the greatest_____ (great) comedian of the silent film era. In

   fact, he attracted _____₁ (large) audiences than

   any other star of his time. Chaplin's _____₂

   (popular) films included *The Gold Rush* (1924), *City Lights* (1931),

   and *Modern Times* (1936). Chaplin has truly been one of the

   _____₃ (well-known) and _____

   _____₄ (well-loved) actors of all times.

2. Marcel Marceau is _____₅ (brilliant) mime of our time. Born in France in 1923, Marceau began his drama studies after World War II. Mime is _____₆ (great) love of his life, and for _____₇ (many) than forty years, he and his mime troupe have enchanted audiences around the world. Marceau's character, Bip, is perhaps his _____ _____₈ (famous) character of all.

■ **EXERCISE C** Complete the following with comparative or superlative forms of the adjectives and adverbs in parentheses. Add *the* when necessary.

1. Georgia O'Keeffe has been *the most famous* _____ (famous) American female artist of the twentieth century.

2. Born on a large farm in Wisconsin in 1887, O'Keeffe felt _____ (much) at home in wide open spaces than she did in cities.

3. Since she had to support herself as a teacher and artist, Georgia O'Keeffe worked _____ (hard) than many other women of her time.

4. It was _____ (difficult) for a woman to be an artist in the 1920s and 1930s than it is today.

5. In her early working years, O'Keeffe received _____ (little) recognition than she deserved.

6. After her marriage to the famous photographer Alfred Stieglitz, O'Keeffe became _____ (well-known).

7. O'Keeffe moved from New York City to New Mexico because she was _____ (happy) in the desert than in a big city.

8. In many ways, life in the desert was _____
   (simple) than in New York.

9. Her _____ (memorable) paintings are, perhaps,
   of desert scenes and of flowers, such as irises.

10. Her paintings of flowers are also some of _____
    (large) and _____ (striking) in her collection.

CLAUSES AND PHRASES SHOWING COMPARISON

Adverb clauses of comparison can be formed with *than* or *as*. In conversational English, these clauses are often shortened to phrases. In formal English, subject pronouns follow *than* or *as*. In informal English, object pronouns are often used, though this is considered incorrect.

Comparative Adjectives and Adverbs

	WITH CLAUSES (MORE FORMAL)	WITH PHRASES (MORE CONVERSATIONAL)
more . . . than *-er . . . than*	I like the theater **more than I like** the movies. I like the theater **more than I do** the movies.	I like the theater **more than** the movies.
less . . . than *-er . . . than*	Maria goes to the theater **less often than I go**. Maria goes to the theater **less often than I (do)**.	Maria goes to the theater **less often than me**.

$\longrightarrow$

Positive Adjectives and Adverbs

	WITH CLAUSES (MORE FORMAL)	WITH PHRASES (MORE CONVERSATIONAL)
as . . . as	Maria likes foreign movies **as much as she likes** American movies. She likes foreign movies **as much as she does** American movies.	Maria likes foreign movies **as much as** American movies.
not as . . . as	Maria says foreign movies **aren't as violent as** American movies are.	Maria says foreign movies **aren't as violent as** American movies. Perhaps foreign movies are **not quite as violent.**

■ **EXERCISE D** Complete the following passage with *as* or *than*.

ALFRED STIEGLITZ AND GEORGIA O'KEEFFE: ART IN THE TWENTIETH CENTURY

Alfred Stieglitz and Georgia O'Keeffe were a brilliantly creative twentieth-century couple. In the beginning of their relationship, Stieglitz was more famous *than* O'Keeffe. Later, she became _____1 famous _____2 he was. Stieglitz was a photographer and O'Keeffe was a painter. Although Stieglitz was much older _____3 she was, their relationship seemed happy. His personality was stronger _____4 hers in the beginning, but as time went on, she became _____5 strong. In their work, she inspired him _____6 much _____7 he inspired her. Together, they produced more creative works _____8 perhaps any other twentieth-century couple.

■ **EXERCISE E** Many comparisons are understood, and the longer form is never given. The following shortened comparisons tell about the early days of two favorite film stars, Mickey Mouse and Donald Duck. Complete each shortened comparison by adding *as* or *than* and the understood comparison.

Example   The original Mickey Mouse had a "mean streak." Today's Mickey Mouse is much nicer.

Today's Mickey Mouse is much nicer than the original was.

1. Mickey Mouse was the star of the first cartoon to use sound — *Steamboat Willie*, in 1928. He produced a storm of "Mousemania" that continues today, and, in fact, few movie characters have been as popular or as well known.
2. The original Mickey Mouse was a troublemaker. Today's Mickey Mouse behaves much better, but he is also more predictable.
3. In the early 1930s, Mickey Mouse was becoming almost too sweet and lovable. Walt Disney decided to create another character who wasn't as nice.
4. In 1934, Donald Duck made his first cartoon appearance, but he looked different from today's Donald. Today's Donald Duck is shorter and rounder. The original Donald was taller and thinner.
5. In his early roles, Donald played the "bad guy" and the "pest." Today's Donald Duck isn't as obnoxious. He also has more depth and more charisma.
6. Mickey Mouse continued to be America's favorite, but by the mid-1930s, Donald was just about as important and beloved. In 1935, the two characters co-starred in *The Band Concert*, their first appearance in Technicolor.

■ **EXERCISE F** In pairs, take turns asking and answering the following questions. As an alternative, choose one of the following as the topic for a short composition.

1. Have you ever seen any silent movies? If you have, tell about them. How are silent films different from "talkies"? What makes them special? Who are your favorite silent film stars and why?
2. If you have never seen any silent films, talk about modern films. Who is your favorite actor? actress? Why?
3. Do you know much about painting? What types of painting are you familiar with? Do you like modern art, or do you prefer more classical styles? Why? Who are some of the best-known painters from your culture?
4. Who is your favorite cartoon character and why? Which American cartoons do you find the funniest? Do you always understand the humor in American cartoons? Is it different from the humor in cartoons in your native language?

PART THREE

Clauses and Related Structures Showing Cause, Contrast, Purpose, and Result or Effect

RHYTHMS AND MOVES

"We are all music makers. Why? Because we are all dreamers of dreams."

—Arthur O'Shaughnessy, 1844–1881

CLAUSES, PHRASES, AND TRANSITIONS SHOWING CAUSE, PURPOSE, AND RESULT OR EFFECT

Cause

TO INTRODUCE CLAUSES

because **since**	**Because** humans need to express their inner feelings, they create works of art.	Most adverb clauses may begin or end sentences. Introductory clauses are generally followed by a comma.

TO INTRODUCE PHRASES

because of **due to**	**Because of** the beauty and creativity of his works, Mozart was considered a musical genius.	Prepositions are followed by phrases, *not* clauses. A comma is generally used after an introductory phrase.

Purpose

TO INTRODUCE CLAUSES

so that	Musicians practice long hours **so that** they can improve their techniques.	*So that* is used only between two clauses. Clauses with *so that* generally use modal auxiliaries (*can, could, may, might, will, would*).

Note: That is sometimes omitted from *so that* in informal English. Do not confuse *so (that)* (meaning purpose) with the conjunction *so* (meaning result). *I went to the store so (that) I could buy bread* (purpose); *I needed bread, so I went to the store* (result).

TO INTRODUCE PHRASES

in order to	Musicians practice long hours **in order to** improve their techniques.	In written English, *in order to* or simply *to* is used more frequently than *so that*.

$\longrightarrow$

Result or Effect

TRANSITIONS

therefore
as a result
for this
   (that)
   reason

Professional dancers need strength as well as grace; **therefore,** they spend long hours exercising.
Professional dancers need to have strong muscles; **for this reason,** they spend a great deal of time doing exercises.

Transitions are words or phrases that link two ideas. They are often used with a semicolon (;), but they can also begin sentences or come at other points in sentences.

■ **EXERCISE A** Complete the following passage by adding *because, because of, since,* or *due to.* Use each expression at least once.

<u>*Because of*</u> his numerous talents, Michael Jackson is one of the most popular entertainers today. _____ his mother and father recognized and encouraged his talent, he is now a

major songwriter, singer, dancer, and actor. _____ most of the nine Jackson children were musically talented, their father, Joe Jackson, formed the family group called "The Jackson Five." The Jackson Five performed as a popular group for many years before breaking up. _____ their natural talent and their parents' encouragement, three of the Jackson children—Michael, Janet, and La Toya—are popular individual performers today. In fact, _____ their tremendous popularity, they often have to travel with bodyguards.

■ **YOUR TURN** What musical groups are popular in your culture today? Why are they popular, and how have they become so? Briefly share information about popular music in your culture and how it has developed.

■ **EXERCISE B** In the following sentences, change *so that* to *in order to* or *in order to* to *so that*.

Example   Rock bands use amplifiers so that they can make their
               music sound louder.
               **Rock bands use amplifiers in order to make their music
               sound louder.**

1. Dancers and singers practice long hours so that they can become successful.
2. Many popular singers take dance lessons so that they can dance well on TV and music videos.
3. Nowadays, dancers and musicians travel a great deal in order to find new rhythms for their music.
4. They travel to Latin America in order to learn rhythms like salsa, samba, and calypso.
5. They travel to Africa so that they can experience the sounds of unusual drumbeats.
6. Dancers and singers blend international rhythms with their own in order to appeal to a larger audience.

■ **EXERCISE C** Combine the following pairs of sentences using *because, since, therefore, as a result,* and *for this reason.* Use each at least once. Change words and add punctuation when necessary.

Example   Music is a very powerful means of expressing ourselves.
               Music has become a means of protest for many groups.
               **Music is a very powerful means of expressing ourselves;
               as a result, it has become a means of protest for many
               groups.**

1. Young Afro-Americans in the cities have created a new type of music. They were angry and needed a new form of expression.
2. This new music is called "rap." It is similar to talking or "rapping" to the sound of drums.
3. Early rap often contained sexist, racist, and combative language. It was not popular with the entire music world.
4. Now some rap is becoming more musical and less combative. It is also becoming more universally acceptable.
5. Performers like M.C. Hammer have added positive messages and great dancing to rap videos. Rap is becoming much more popular.

■ **YOUR TURN** Is music a form of protest in your culture? If so, what does it protest and why? If music is not a form of protest, or if protest music is only a small part of popular music in your culture, what does music usually express for your culture and why?

CLAUSES, PHRASES, AND TRANSITIONS SHOWING CONTRAST — CONCESSION AND OPPOSITION
Concession

The following clauses, phrases, and transitions are used to express ideas and information that are different from our expectations.

TO INTRODUCE CLAUSES		
although even though though	**Although** many artists work long and hard, not all of them are successful.	These conjunctions are commonly used in speaking and writing, but *although* is preferred in formal English.

TO INTRODUCE PHRASES		
despite in spite of	**Despite** years of practice, only a few artists make it to the top.	*Despite* and *in spite of* are followed by phrases, not clauses. The phrases may contain nouns, pronouns, or gerunds.

$\longrightarrow$

however	Many people dream of being professional musicians or dancers; **however,** it is often difficult for artists to make a decent living. Many people dream of being professional musicians or dancers; it is often difficult for artists to make a decent living, **however.**	*However* is frequently used in both speaking and writing. It may appear at the beginning or end or in the middle of a sentence.

Opposition

The following clauses, phrases, and transitions are used to express an opposite view of the same idea or information.

TO INTRODUCE CLAUSES

where **while**	**While** some artists become successful during their lifetimes, others achieve fame only after death. Some artists become successful during their lifetimes, **where** others achieve fame only after death.	*Where* and *while* are usually used to contrast direct opposites. In many cases, the connecting word may begin either clause. The focus of the sentence changes but not the meaning.

TO INTRODUCE PHRASES

instead of	**Instead of** achieving wealth and fame, Van Gogh died in poverty.	*Instead of* is followed by a noun phrase or a gerund, not a clause.

TRANSITIONS

in contrast **on the other hand**	Van Gogh died in poverty; **in contrast,** Picasso lived as a multi-millionaire.	*In contrast* and *on the other hand* relate different points that are not necessarily direct opposites.

■ **EXERCISE D** Combine the following pairs of sentences with *although, even though, though,* and *however.* Use each at least once. Be sure to change or omit words and to add punctuation when necessary.

Example   "Beatlemania" had swept through Europe in 1963. The Beatles did not become popular in the U.S. until the following year.
        Although "Beatlemania" had swept through Europe in 1963, the Beatles did not become popular in the U.S. until the following year.

1. At the beginning of 1964, most Americans had never heard of the Beatles. Within six weeks, millions were listening to the Beatles.
2. Many parents disapproved of the Beatles, especially their hair. American teenagers went wild over the Beatles.
3. Most pop music groups had one star. All four Beatles were major stars with distinct personalities and talents.
4. The Beatles had a tremendous amount of natural talent. They did not have any formal musical training.
5. Some songs were better than others. Almost every single recording was a hit.

■ **EXERCISE E** Two of this century's most creative musicians have been the jazz greats Louis Armstrong and Miles Davis. Both played horns, but in other aspects, they were two very different individuals. Read the information about them below. Then form sentences with *where, while, in contrast,* or *on the other hand.* Use each connecting word at least once.

Example   Louis Armstrong always tried to please his audiences and his fans.
Miles Davis did not seem to care about popularity.
Louis Armstrong always tried to please his audiences and his fans; in contrast, Miles Davis did not seem to care about popularity.

1. Armstrong came from a relatively poor family in New Orleans.

   Miles Davis was born into a prosperous middle-class family in East Saint Louis.

2. Louis Armstrong was friendly and fun-loving.

   Miles Davis was often called mysterious, rebellious, and even shy.

3. Armstrong was a film star and comedian as well as a musician.

   Davis concentrated only on jazz.

4. Armstrong maintained a consistent style throughout his career.

   Miles Davis changed his musical style numerous times.

5. There is a simplicity and clarity to most of Louis Armstrong's music.

   The music of Miles Davis is often very abstract and complex.

■ **YOUR TURN** Can you think of two musicians in your culture who have different styles and different personalities? If so, tell your classmates a little about these people — their personalities, their lifestyles, their politics, and their music.

■ **EXERCISE F** Martha Graham was an amazingly creative dancer and choreographer. In fact, she helped create the whole realm of modern dance in the United States. Complete the following sentences about her with *instead of, despite, although, though,* and *while*. Use each at least once.

1. *Although* _____ she was considered "too old," Martha Graham began her professional dance career at age twenty-two.

2. _____ letting her age stop her, she fought hard to become a professional dancer.

3. Martha Graham was generally regarded as kind, humorous, and generous, _____ her quick and violent temper.

4. Graham gave the appearance of great stature and force on stage, _____ she was, in fact, a very tiny woman.

5. _____ some of her dances were about the United States, much of her work was inspired by Greek dramas, stories, and myths.

6. _____ the times and places of her settings vary, Martha Graham's dances almost always involved human conflicts and emotions.

7. Graham always tried to create new and different movements _____ heavy criticism at different times in her career.

8. _____ following tradition, Graham was constantly innovative throughout her long career.

■ **EXERCISE G Review of Connecting Words** Complete the following passage with these connecting words and phrases: *after, although, because, because of, but, despite, due to, however, instead of, since, so that, when,* and *while.* Use each connecting word or phrase at least once.

JULIO IGLESIAS

Because _____ Julio Iglesias is a very popular international singer and songwriter, most people consider him lucky. *However* , _____₁ he was younger, he wasn't so lucky. Iglesias had started a promising career as a soccer player (goalie) for *Real Madrid Club de Fútbol* in Spain. _____₂ he had been successful, professional soccer was not meant to be his career. _____₃ a serious car accident that almost killed him, Julio was forced to change professions.

After his accident, Julio spent a year in a hospital. _____₄ he was recovering, he learned to play the guitar. A nurse had given him an inexpensive guitar _____₅ he would have something to occupy his time in the hospital. _____₆ he was learning to play the guitar by listening to the radio, he also discovered his ability to sing.

_____₇ Julio had finally left the hospital, he started a career in law. At that time, he was considering becoming a lawyer; _____₈, music attracted him much more. In the end, _____₉ his interest in a career as a lawyer, he decided to devote himself to music _____₁₀ law.

Perhaps it is possible that Julio Iglesias could still be a good lawyer, _____11 he certainly has done well with music. _____12 he began his musical career, he has attracted millions of fans worldwide. Unfortunately, his soccer career was ended by a bad injury and bad luck. _____13 his injury, Julio was able to find music. A strange kind of luck!

PART   FOUR

Clauses of Time — Past Time

CREATIVITY AND GENIUS IN SCIENCE

When Albert Einstein was a child, his parents actually suspected that he was mentally retarded. And after he had graduated from a technical school, he could not find a teaching position in science. Yet Einstein became one of the world's greatest scientists, and today his name is synonymous with genius.

ADVERB CLAUSES OF TIME—PAST TIME WITH THE SIMPLE PAST AND PAST CONTINUOUS TENSES

when	**When** Einstein **had** time during the workday, he **wrote** down his ideas.	The simple past is used with *when* to show a direct connection in time of occurrence.
while	**While** he **was working** in the patent office, he **had** plenty of time to think.	The past continuous is used in time clauses to express past actions in progress at a particular time.
as	**As** he **was working,** he **was** also **thinking.**	

■ **EXERCISE A** Complete the following passage by using simple past or past continuous forms of the verbs in parentheses. Include adverbs where indicated.

ALBERT EINSTEIN

When Einstein _was_ (be) a child, he _____1 (show) no early evidence of genius. While he _____2 (learn) to talk, he _____3 (have) tremendous difficulties, and his parents _____4 (suspect / even) him of being mentally retarded. In high school, he _____5 (be) an average student. When he _____6 (graduate / finally) from a technical institute in Zurich, Switzerland, he _____7 (not be) able to find a teaching appointment in science. He _____8 (end) up working in a patent office in Bern, Switzerland.

Einstein _____9 (not want) that type of job, but as he _____10 (work) in the office, he _____11 (be) able to spend time thinking. Several years later he _____12 (publish) five papers in one year, 1905. These papers _____13 (include) an explanation of his special theory of relativity, which _____14 (begin) a worldwide scientific revolution.

ADVERB CLAUSES OF TIME—PAST TIME WITH THE SIMPLE PAST AND PAST PERFECT TENSES

before **by the time** **(that)** **until** **when**	Leonardo da Vinci **had painted** the Mona Lisa **before** he **worked** on many of his ideas for inventions.	In sentences with time clauses, the past perfect is used to refer to an event or situation that came before another event or time in the past. With *before, by the time that, until,* and *when,* the past perfect is used in the main clause.
already **hardly** **just** **scarcely** **not . . .** **yet**	Leonardo da Vinci **had already worked** as a civil engineer, military engineer, and architect **by the time** he **began** his major paintings.	Adverbs such as *already, hardly, just, scarcely,* and *not . . . yet* are often used with the past perfect. They generally come between *had* and the past participle.
after **as soon as**	**After** Leonardo da Vinci **had painted** his major artworks, he **spent** more time on his inventions.	In complex sentences with *after* and *as soon as,* the past perfect (continuous) is used in the dependent (not the main) clause.

Note: After, before, by, and *until* can also be used as prepositions in phrases of time. Sentences with *before, by,* and *until* may use the past perfect tense, while sentences with *after* would generally use the simple past tense.

Subordinating conjunction	**Before** he began his major paintings, da Vinci had already worked as an engineer and architect. **After** da Vinci had painted many of his major artworks, he spent more time on his inventions.
Preposition	**Before** 1495, da Vinci had already worked as an engineer and architect. **After** 1500, da Vinci spent more time on his inventions.

■ **EXERCISE B** Everyone develops special talents during his or her lifetime, but few are able to equal the extraordinary achievements of the following individuals. Complete the passages by using simple past or past perfect forms (active or passive) of the verbs in parentheses. Note any case where you feel both tenses are appropriate.

1. **Leonardo da Vinci**

   Most people recognize Leonardo da Vinci as the painter of the *Mona Lisa* and the *Last Supper*, but he _was also_____ (be / also) a master of design, engineering, science, and invention. After da Vinci _had painted_____ (paint) his most famous works, he _____1 (spend) more time on his other ideas. In physics, da Vinci _____2 (discover) many complex physical principles nearly a century before Galileo _____3 (confirm) them. In anatomy, da Vinci _____4 (develop) a theory on the circulation of blood a century before William Harvey _____5 (prove) it.

2. **Johann Wolfgang von Goethe**

   Goethe _____6 (live) from 1749 to 1832. He _____7 (be) a scientist as well as the greatest of German poets. By age sixteen, _____8 (write / already) religious poems, a novel, and a prose epic. While continuing to write, he _____9 (study) both law and medicine. After he _____10 (invite) to live in Weimar, Germany, he _____11 (become) minister of state. Because of his position, he _____12 (educate) himself in agriculture, horticulture, and mining. He then _____13 (proceed) to master anatomy, biology, optics, and mineralogy.

3. **Margaret Mead**

   By the time Margaret Mead _____14 (turn) twenty-six, she _____15 (name / already) curator of the American Museum of Natural History. Before she _____₁₆ (reach) thirty, she _____₁₇ (publish) two major books about her studies of the people of Oceania. Before her death in 1978, she _____₁₈ (write) hundreds of articles and books on topics ranging from anthropology to nuclear warfare and disarmament.

■ **YOUR TURN** Is there someone you particularly admire for his or her knowledge or accomplishments? He or she may be a scientist, an artist, a musician, a sports figure, a politician, and/or a friend. What did this person do? How did the person accomplish this? Give a brief description of these accomplishments in chronological order.

■ **EXERCISE C** Below is information about Thomas Edison and some of his accomplishments. The pairs of sentences are listed in chronological order. Use the cues in parentheses to combine each pair. Use a past perfect verb in each new sentence. Change nouns, and adverbs, omit words, and add punctuation when necessary.

Example   Thomas Edison ended his formal education.
          Thomas Edison became a teenager. (long before)
          Thomas Edison had ended his formal education long before he became a teenager.

1. Thomas Edison invented dozens of practical tools and machines.
   Thomas Edison reached his early twenties. (before / already)
2. Edison made some money from an invention for the stock market.
   Edison set up a factory in Newark, New Jersey. (soon after)
3. Edison ran the factory for just two years.
   Edison decided to organize the first U.S. industrial research park in Menlo Park, New Jersey. (when)
4. In his attempts to create a light bulb, Edison tried hundreds of metal combinations.
   Edison finally found the right one to conduct electricity. (before)
5. Edison developed the first commercial light bulb.
   Edison created the mimeograph, dictating machines, early motion-picture cameras and projectors, and an iron-alkaline battery, among other inventions. (after)
6. Edison received over 1,000 patents for practical applications of scientific principles.
   Edison died. (by the time that)

■ **YOUR TURN** Use information from Exercise C and gather more information at your library to write a short composition on Edison and his accomplishments.

■ **EXERCISE D** Below you will find information on Marie Curie and the discovery of radium. Marie Curie is the only person in history to win two Nobel Prizes in science. Complete the passage by using simple past, past continuous, or past perfect forms (active or passive) of the verbs in parentheses.

1. Born in Poland in 1867, Marie Sklodowska _was not allowed_ (allow / not) to attend school beyond the high-school level.

2. After an older brother and sister _____ (leave) for a university education in Paris, Marie _____ (work) to send them money and to save for her own education.

3. While she _____ (work), Marie _____ (teach) herself from family books.

4. As soon as she _____ (save) enough money, she _____ (go / also) to Paris.

5. While Marie _____ (study) at the Sorbonne, she _____ (live) as economically as possible and _____ (spend) all of her time studying.

6. When she _____ (graduate), Marie Sklodowska _____ (be) at the top of her class.

7. In 1894, she _____ (introduce) to Pierre Curie. Curie _____ (become / already) somewhat famous for his work in physics.

8. After Marie _____ (marry) Pierre Curie, she _____ (begin) to apply his earlier discoveries to the measurement of radioactivity.

9. Scarcely six years after Marie _____ (arrive) in Paris, she _____ (make) major discoveries about radioactivity. Pierre _____ (see) the potential and _____ (drop) his own research to join her.

10. In December 1898, the Curies _____ (conduct)

 other experiments with uranium ore when they

 _____ (detect) a new radioactive substance,

 radium.

11. In 1903, Marie Curie _____ (write) her disserta-

 tion on radioactivity, and, for it, she and Pierre _____

 _____ (give) that year's Nobel Prize in physics with Antoine

 Becquerel.

12. After Pierre Curie's death in 1906, Marie _____

 (continue) her study of radioactive elements, and in 1911, she

 _____ (award) the Nobel Prize in chemistry.

■ **YOUR TURN** Use information from the preceding exercise to write a short paragraph about Marie Curie.

■ **EXERCISE E Review of Adverb Clauses** Complete the following passage with connecting words such as *after, as, as a result, by the time that, due to, even though, however, in order to, in spite of, since, so that, until, when, while,* or any others that are appropriate.

MAGIC MACHINES

Melea Rodgers is a lawyer in Decatur, Alabama. *When* _____

she arrives at work each day, she opens the morning mail. _____

_____ ₁, she does not read her mail by herself. A voice from a

briefcase-size machine, a Kurzweil Personal Reader, reads it to her.

 Melea Rodgers suffers from diabetes; _____ ₂,

she went blind several years ago. _____ ₃ she

received her Kurzweil Personal Reader, she had depended on others to

read to her. Now her Kurzweil can read aloud to her in any of nine

distinct voice styles. "_____ ₄ I got my Kurzweil last

year, I've been on my own. It's a wonderful feeling," says Rodgers.

The Kurzweil is named after Raymond Kurzweil. _____

_____5 his incredible talent, Kurzweil is considered one of the most remarkable inventors alive. A soft-spoken businessman scientist from Waltham, Massachusetts, Kurzweil has repeatedly astonished colleagues and competitors alike with his "smart machines."

_____6 he was growing up in New York, Kurzweil became an accomplished magician. Then he discovered computers. _____7 he turned sixteen, he had written a computer program for the IBM Corporation.

Kurzweil went on to college, and _____8 he had graduated from M.I.T., he worked on his inventions. He created a computer able to read printed text and speak the words through a voice-synthesizing unit.

During this time, Kurzweil had major problems with money, and he even sold his car and tape recorders _____9 he could pay his bills. Then his luck began to change. In 1976, he appeared on television _____10 demonstrate his special machine. Blind singer Stevie Wonder was listening to the program and immediately traveled to Massachusetts _____11 he could meet the inventor. "He wanted one right away," Kurzweil recalls. "_____12 that first machine weighed about 350 pounds and cost $50,000, we loaded it right into his car." Wonder stayed up all that night reading. He says that the machine has been "a brother and a friend."

Today Ray Kurzweil is working on new and different machines such as his Kurzweil music synthesizer, which is used by top stars like Stevie Wonder and Kenny Rodgers. _____13 his current success, Kurzweil has not forgotten his roots. "_____14 I was a boy," he says, "I loved to perform magic tricks, and I loved the look of delight on people's faces ————————————₁₅ they saw something impossible happen. ————————————₁₆ I grew older, I simply discovered a more powerful form of magic—the computer."

Language Activities

These speaking and writing activities are designed to help you practice the many different connecting words and phrases covered in this chapter.

CLAUSES OF TIME—PRESENT OR FUTURE TIME

■ **ACTIVITY A** Who is someone that you consider creative? Do you have a friend or relative who is good at making or fixing things, at painting, at cooking or baking, or at playing or writing music? Give a brief presentation on a creative individual you know. Use the following questions to help you prepare.

1. How is this person creative?
2. When is he or she the most creative? What seems to inspire him or her?
3. Has this person always been creative?
4. What interesting things has he or she done or produced?
5. What is this person doing now? Is he or she still involved in creative activities?

■ **ACTIVITY B** Think about the various descriptions of creativity and problem-solving in this chapter. Try to put these ideas to use as you consider the problems of teaching and learning a language. Imagine that you and your classmates are educational consultants. You have been asked to design a program for a private language school.

Separate into small groups. Discuss your ideas on the best ways to learn languages. Then, as a group, make a list of recommendations for planning a language program. Be sure to consider the following and to add any of your own ideas.

1. How many students should there be per class? How many different teachers should students have?

2. How many hours a day should students have classes? When should the classes be offered?
3. What kinds of classes should be offered?
4. Should there be a language lab? Should use of the lab be optional or mandatory?

Remember that both money and time may be problems for the students. Some may be working. Some may have families. Many will not be able to afford expensive classes. How should you plan if you want to offer economical and effective classes?

■ **ACTIVITY C**   Rube Goldberg was a creative American cartoonist. He "created" some of the world's most amazing "inventions." The invention in the accompanying cartoon is designed to attract a waiter's attention. Read the text and then follow the drawing to give the step-by-step process involved. Use *if, when, before,* and *after* to join the steps.

Example   **If you light the skyrocket, the skyrocket will go off. When the skyrocket goes off, the string will open the jack-in-the-box. When the jack-in-the-box opens, . . .**

COMPARISONS

■ **ACTIVITY D**   What movies or plays have you seen this year? What books have you read? What concerts have you gone to? Vote on *the best* and *the worst* of 199_. Choose several categories and then list your choices. Take a vote in the class and then give your results. As an alternative, you may want to cover movies or TV programs only and use categories such as the saddest, the funniest, the most violent, the least interesting, or the most inspiring.

■ **ACTIVITY E** Choose two or three of your own favorite creative personalities. They may be movie stars, musicians, sports figures, singers or songwriters, painters, or politicians. In a composition, briefly describe the work of each. Then make comparisons, giving your own opinion on which you prefer and why. After you have written your composition, tell your classmates about it in small groups.

CLAUSES AND PHRASES OF CAUSE, CONTRAST, PURPOSE, RESULT OR EFFECT, AND TIME

■ **ACTIVITY F** M. C. Escher was a Dutch artist who lived from 1902 to 1972. He created some of the most unusual and stimulating drawings in history. The drawing on the left is his interpretation of relativity. In pairs or in small groups, discuss the following questions about this work. Be sure to include your own questions too.

1. How do you react when you see a drawing like this?
2. Try to imagine what Escher was thinking about while he was planning this.
3. Why do you think he called it *Relativity*?
4. How do you think he drew the picture? For example, do you think he drew several separate pictures and later put them together?

■ **ACTIVITY G** Leonardo da Vinci was "far ahead of his time." He had drawn plans for a number of inventions that were not developed until centuries later. Some of these plans included an airplane, an elevator, a helicopter, lock gates for canals, a submarine, and a tank. In small groups, discuss one or more of these inventions. Try to imagine what da Vinci had been thinking, doing, or feeling before he created his plans and how he arrived at them. You might want to use the following questions to help you. After you have finished, choose one member to give a brief summary for the class.

1. What do you think led da Vinci to these ideas? What problems had he been trying to solve?
2. Can you think of any reasons he didn't develop the actual invention? (He *did* design and build a type of gate for canal locks.) Were all the necessary materials available at that time?
3. When were these inventions actually developed?
4. How have they changed since then?
5. How have they affected our lives?

CHAPTER 7

Human Behavior

Adjective Clauses

In this chapter, you will study complex sentences with another type of clause, the adjective clause. As you study the chapter, pay attention to the different relative pronouns used with adjective clauses and to the role of punctuation in their meanings.

Previewing the Passage

What makes humans different from animals? What makes one person different from another? In what ways are we the same?

Understanding Human Nature

Why do we act the way we do? How do we learn to act in certain ways? How should we cope with problems? How can we find happiness and peace? What is the best way to live? What gives our life
5   meaning?

These are questions that people have asked throughout history. Philosophers, psychologists, medical doctors, sociologists, physiologists, anthropologists, and physicists are among the many
10 thinkers who have tried to give us answers.

Researchers who have worked long hours on the puzzles of our lives tell us bits and pieces about us and our behavior — why we sleep or don't sleep, why we get angry easily or why we're easy-
15 going, how we learn. They tell us about everything from language to complex mathematics.

For many, science and scientific research are the keys that will unlock the secrets of humans. Their hope is that scientists who study the body and brain will give us answers to all our questions about life. And perhaps scientists will.
20 For others, however, it is religion that gives many of the answers to these questions.

Whether through science or religion or through both, all cultures in the world make interpretations of human nature. All cultures give suggestions or make rules on how to act. Despite the variety of approaches, all cultures are pursuing
25 the same goal, understanding our nature and guiding our behavior. In the end, will we ever understand ourselves? According to a Malaysian proverb, "The deep sea can be fathomed, but who knows the hearts and minds of men?"

Understanding Vocabulary

1. The suffix *-logy* comes from a Greek word meaning "reason." Today it means "the study of." Combine the following with the suffix *-logy*. Then try to give an explanation of that area of study.

    anthropo- from Greek, meaning "humans" or "a period of human existence"

    bio- from Greek, meaning "life" or "living matter"

physio- from both Greek and Latin, meaning "nature" or "appearance"

psycho- from Greek, meaning "of the mind"

socio- from Latin, meaning "companion or associate"

zoo- from Greek, meaning "living being" or "animal"

2. The suffix *-ist* also comes from Greek, and it means "one who makes or performs." In many cases, it means "someone who studies." Use the areas of study determined above to form words with *-ist*. Then complete these sentences with the correct names of the scientists.

    a. Chang is studying the culture, customs, and beliefs of humans.

       He is an _____ .

    b. Joan is doing research on photosynthesis in plants. She is a

       _____ .

    c. Ali is studying white rhinoceroses in Africa. He is a

       _____ .

    d. Antonio is completing his thesis on memory and dreams. He is a

       _____ .

    e. Dr. Ito is researching problems of humans in digesting red meat.

       She is a _____ .

    f. Rita is studying the effects of poverty on crime in urban areas.

       She is a _____ .

Discussing Ideas

1. In your opinion, what makes humans different from animals?
2. Science and philosophy or religion have often been viewed as in conflict. In your opinion, must there be a conflict between the two?
3. Who do you think can give us the best answers as to why we are the way we are and how we should live?

P A R T   O N E

Adjective Clauses with *That, When,* and *Where*—Replacement of Subjects, Objects, and Adverbials of Time or Place

CONSCIOUSNESS AND "ALTERED STATES"

Consciousness is the awareness that people have of their actions. In contrast, an altered state is a time when we lose our awareness. Sleeping and dreaming are examples of altered states that everyone experiences.

ADJECTIVE CLAUSES

An adjective clause is a clause that modifies a noun or pronoun. An adjective clause usually comes immediately after the word(s) it modifies. In some cases, a pronoun or prepositional phrase may come between the noun or pronoun and the clause.

Adjective Clauses with *That*—Replacement of Subjects

That can replace the subject of a simple sentence. It is used for ideas and things. In informal English, *that* is sometimes used to refer to people; *who* is generally preferred, however. Commas are *not* used with adjective clauses beginning with *that.*

Simple sentences	Sleep is a complex (process.) (This process) occurs in several distinct stages.
Complex sentence	Sleep is a complex process **that** occurs in several distinct stages.
Simple sentences	There are a few unusual (people.) (These people) need only three or four hours of sleep each night.
Complex sentence	There are a few unusual people **that (who)** need only three or four hours of sleep each night.

■ **EXERCISE A** Combine the following sentences to form adjective clauses with *that*. Make any necessary changes in your new sentences. Then show any cases where *who* is also appropriate.

Example In the early 1970s, there were some researchers. These researchers studied the personalities of "short sleepers" and "long sleepers."
In the early 1970s, there were some researchers that (who) studied the personalities of "short sleepers" and "long sleepers."

1. In the early 1970s, several researchers conducted experiments. These experiments compared personalities and sleeping habits.
2. "Short sleepers" are people. They need less than 6½ hours of sleep.
3. According to the 1970s research, people tend to be short sleepers. They have a lot of energy.
4. In contrast, "long sleepers" are individuals. They need more than 8½ hours of sleep each night.
5. According to the 1970s research, people are often long sleepers. They worry a lot.
6. Recent experiments did not find any personality differences between "short" and "long" sleepers. These recent experiments repeated the same studies.

■ **YOUR TURN** How many hours of sleep do you need each night? Are you a short sleeper or a long sleeper? Do you have a lot of energy? Do you worry much? Compare your answers with those of your classmates. Do the class's answers seem to support the findings from the 1970s or the more recent ones?

Adjective Clauses with *When* and *Where* — Replacement of Adverbials of Time or Place

When and *where* can be used as relative pronouns that replace adverbials of time or place. Do not confuse adjective clauses with *when* or *where* (which follow the noun[s] they modify) with adverb clauses (which may begin or end sentences).

Simple sentences	REM (Rapid-Eye-Movement) sleep is (a time.) We dream (then.)
Complex sentence	REM sleep is the time **when** we dream.
Simple sentences	A sleep laboratory is (a place.) The stages of sleep are studied (there.)
Complex sentence	A sleep laboratory is a place **where** the stages of sleep are studied.

■ **EXERCISE B** Below is information on the various stages of sleep. The information is written in the form of notes. Expand the notes into complete sentences with *when*. Make any necessary changes.

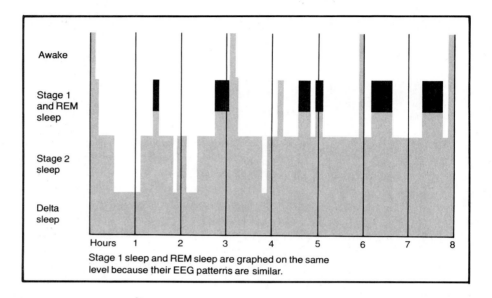

Hours 1 2 3 4 5 6 7 8

Stage 1 sleep and REM sleep are graphed on the same level because their EEG patterns are similar.

Example   NREM sleep: we are not dreaming
NREM sleep is the time when we are not dreaming.

1. *Stage 1: we lose awareness of our surroundings*

2. *Stage 1: our thoughts begin to drift, but we're not completely asleep*

3. *Stage 2: we're finally fully asleep*

4. *Delta sleep: we enter our deepest sleep, and it is most difficult to wake us*

5. *REM sleep: our eyes begin to move rapidly*

6. *REM sleep: we are dreaming*

Adjective Clauses with *That*—Replacement of Objects of Verbs

To form an adjective clause, the relative pronoun *that* can replace the object of the verb in a simple sentence. *That* generally refers to things or ideas, and in informal English, it may be used to refer to people. In addition, *that* is sometimes omitted in informal English; this is possible only when *that* replaces an object (not the subject).

⟶

Simple sentences	The (basic sleep stages) are NREM* and REM†. Normal sleepers go through (these stages.)
Complex sentences	The basic sleep stages **that** normal sleepers go through are NREM* and REM† or The basic sleep stages normal sleepers go through are NREM* and REM†.

---

* *Non-Rapid-Eye-Movement*   During most sleeping time, your eyes do not move.
† *Rapid-Eye-Movement*   While you are dreaming, your eyes move very rapidly.

■ **EXERCISE C**   Combine each pair of sentences with *that*. Then combine the sentences without *that*.

Example   The machine is called an EEG, or an electroencephalogram. Sleep researchers use this machine to measure brain waves.
The machine that sleep researchers use to measure brain waves is called an EEG.
The machine sleep researchers use to measure brain waves is called an EEG.

1. The EEG is a machine. Researchers use this machine to measure waves in our brains.
2. The brain waves are different in every stage of sleep. The EEG records the brain waves.
3. Most of the stages belong to a general category called NREM (Non-Rapid-Eye-Movement). People pass through these stages.
4. The rest of the time is in REM (Rapid-Eye-Movement) sleep. We spend this time sleeping.
5. Generally the sleep is 80 percent NREM and 20 percent REM. We get this sleep each night.
6. The amount of REM sleep is very important. We get REM sleep each night.

■ **EXERCISE D**   Complete the following sentences with *that, when,* or *where,* or use *X* to indicate that no connecting word is necessary. Give all possibilities for each sentence.

Example   REM sleep is the stage *when* _____ dreams are most vivid and most easily remembered.

1. Research _____ involves sleeping habits can often be very complicated.

2. Universities are the places _____ most sleep research is done today.

3. REM sleep is a time _____ the brain is extremely active, but the body is almost totally still.

4. The average number of hours _____ the average person spends dreaming each night is about 1½.

5. According to some psychologists, the dreams _____ people report may say something about their subconscious* desires or needs.

6. For example, a dream _____ people experience more than once or twice is called a recurring dream.

7. In many recurring dreams _____ college students reported, the dreamers were being threatened or pursued, and they were trying to hide.

8. The students reported these dreams at a time _____ they were worried about something in their lives.

■ **YOUR TURN** Have you ever had a recurring dream? What was it about? Could you link it to something that was happening in your life at the time? If you have had this experience, briefly tell or write about it.

■ **EXERCISE E Error Analysis** Many of the following sentences have errors in the formation of adjective clauses. Find and correct the errors. Indicate sentences that have no errors.

1. Insomnia is a problem ~~where~~ *that or x* many people have.

2. Insomnia is a sleep disorder that involves difficulty in going to sleep or in staying asleep for the night.

3. People that they suffer from insomnia use many methods to treat it.

4. Tranquilizers are drugs that some people take them to sleep better.

5. People that they can't sleep well are called insomniacs.

6. Insomniacs must learn to avoid thoughts or behaviors interfere with their sleep.

---

* *subconscious* something existing in our mind that we are not aware of

7. If you are an insomniac, evening is a time then you should relax and have fun, not work or deal with problems.

8. Your bed is not a place that you should worry about your problems.

PART TWO

Restrictive and Nonrestrictive Clauses; Clauses with *Who, Which,* and *Whose*— Replacement of Subjects and Possessives

LANGUAGE AND LANGUAGE LEARNING

How do children around the world learn language at such an early age? Scientists who have studied language development have proposed two theories: the genetic theory, which states that children are "programmed" to learn language before birth, and the environmental theory, which emphasizes the importance of learning, observation, and imitation.

RESTRICTIVE AND NONRESTRICTIVE ADJECTIVE CLAUSES

Restrictive clauses identify the nouns they describe. No commas are used with restrictive clauses.

Nonrestrictive clauses do *not* define or identify the nouns they describe. Nonrestrictive clauses give *extra* information. A comma is used at the beginning and at the end of a nonrestrictive clause. *That* may not be used with nonrestrictive clauses (with commas).

Restrictive	I met a scientist **who was interested in language acquisition**.	Restrictive clauses explain *which* people, places, things, or ideas—not everyone or everything, only what is described in the clause.
Nonrestrictive	I met Professor Chang, **who was interested in language acquisition**.	Nonrestrictive clauses add extra information about the noun(s). They do *not* explain *which* people (places, things, etc.). The identity of the noun is already known. Clauses that modify proper names, entire groups, or nouns that are unique (the sun, sky, etc.) are generally nonrestrictive.

In some cases, the same clause may either identify or give extra information, depending on the situation.

Restrictive	My brother **who lives in Oregon** is a teacher. (I have several brothers; the brother in Oregon is a teacher.)	This clause tells *which* brother. No commas are used.
Nonrestrictive	My brother, **who lives in Oregon,** is a teacher. (I have only one brother, or I'm talking about one brother now. By the way, he lives in Oregon.)	This clause gives extra information. Commas are used.

$\longrightarrow$

Note: In spoken English, speakers often pause before and after a nonrestrictive clause. This tells you that the information is extra. Thus pauses are likely in the second sentence but not in the first.

■ **EXERCISE A** As your teacher reads the following sentences aloud, underline the adjective clause in each. Then decide whether the information is *essential* (telling *which* person, thing, etc.) or *extra*. Add commas if the information is extra.

Example The ability to speak is a unique behavior <u>which separates humans from all other animals.</u>
Essential information, no commas

1. The ability to speak which separates humans from all other animals may be present at birth.
2. Some researchers who study language development believe we are born with the ability to learn language.
3. Noam Chomsky who is one of the most famous linguists of our time believes in a genetic* ability to learn language.
4. As proof, Chomsky says children can produce sentences which are completely original.
5. Children create sentences which they have never heard before.
6. Our son Martin who is three creates very unusual sentences all the time.
7. Other scientists who have studied the development of children believe in the "imitation" theory.
8. According to them, language is learned more slowly by children who don't have many opportunities to listen to and imitate other people.
9. In any case, childhood seems to be the time when it is easiest to learn languages.
10. My cousin who was born in Poland learned English, Polish, and French as a child. (I have only one cousin.)
11. John's cousin who was born in Poland speaks four languages fluently. (John has many cousins.)

---

* *genetic* hereditary, part of our biochemistry at birth

ADJECTIVE CLAUSES WITH *WHO* AND *WHICH* — REPLACEMENT OF SUBJECTS

To form an adjective clause, the relative pronoun *who* or *which* can replace the subject of a simple sentence. *Who* refers to people only. It may be used in both restrictive and nonrestrictive clauses. *Which* refers to things or ideas. In nonrestrictive clauses (with commas), *which* (not *that*) must be used. In restrictive clauses (without commas), either *which* or *that* may be used, but *that* is preferred.

Simple sentences	We spoke with Professor Chang. Professor Chang is a Chinese psychologist.
Complex sentence	We spoke with Professor Chang, **who** is a Chinese psychologist.
Simple sentences	Professor Chang will talk about his specialty. His specialty is the study of language acquisition in children.
Complex sentence	Professor Chang will lecture on his specialty, **which** is the study of language acquisition in children.

■ **EXERCISE B** In the following sentences, decide whether you may change *who* or *which* to *that*. If you can, make the change. If you cannot, explain why not.

Example In some parts of the United States, there are children who grow up speaking two languages.

In some parts of the United States, there are children that grow up speaking two languages.

1. Children who grow up speaking two languages are bilingual.
2. Bilingualism, which is somewhat unusual in the United States, is very common in many other countries.
3. Along the Vaupés River in South America, almost two dozen different languages are spoken in a small area which is populated by about ten thousand Indians.

NOW HERE'S A BAD JOKE. IF SOMEONE WHO SPEAKS TWO LANGUAGES IS BILINGUAL, AND SOMEONE WHO SPEAKS THREE LANGUAGES IS TRILINGUAL WHAT'S A PERSON WHO SPEAKS ONLY ONE LANGUAGE?

AN AMERICAN!

4. According to the traditions of this region, people *must* find mates who do not speak their language.
5. All the children who grow up in this region speak at least three languages: their mother's, their father's, and the lingua franca* of the region.
6. Tukano, which is the lingua franca of the Vaupés region, has been studied by several linguists.
7. Similarly, almost everyone is bilingual or trilingual in countries that have more than one official national language, like Switzerland and India.
8. Other examples include Filipinos, who often use English as their lingua franca, and East Africans, who generally use Swahili as their lingua franca.

■ **YOUR TURN** Do people in your culture use a *lingua franca*? If so, tell your classmates about it.

■ **EXERCISE C** Use *who* or *which* to form an adjective clause from the second sentence in each pair. Combine the sentences, omitting words and adding commas when necessary.

Example All over the world, children pass through several distinct stages. They are learning to talk.
All over the world, children who are learning to talk pass through several distinct stages.

1. In the first stage, children produce random† sounds. These sounds are called babbling.
2. By nine months, the baby begins making sounds. These sounds resemble the vowels and consonants of the language.
3. The child's first words usually refer to things in the child's world, for example, *mama, milk,* or *cat.* The child's first words appear around age one.
4. At about age two, the child can form two-word sentences such as *Where's doggie?* or *Me play.* The child now has a vocabulary of more than fifty words.
5. Children have already learned the general rules of grammar for their language, as well as the exceptions. These children are entering school.

---

* *lingua franca* a language used for common communication in areas where people speak many individual languages or dialects
† *random* accidental, not on purpose

6. Children also learn to recognize and understand facial expressions and gestures at a very early age. All children are very sensitive to changes in voice and posture.
7. A few children never learn to speak perfectly. These children have not been exposed to speech by the age of ten or eleven.
8. On the other hand, Charles Berlitz learned four different languages as a child. Charles Berlitz later specialized in language education.

■ **YOUR TURN**   Have you ever observed a small child who was learning to talk? Perhaps it was your own child, a young relative, or the child of a friend. Can you remember anything that the child said or did? What stage do you think he or she was in? Share your answers with your classmates.

ADJECTIVE CLAUSES WITH *WHOSE*— REPLACEMENT OF POSSESSIVES

The relative pronoun *whose* can be used to form an adjective clause. It replaces a possessive. *Whose* generally refers to people, but it may also refer to places, ideas, or things.

Simple sentences	I never miss a class with (Professor Chang.) (Professor Chang's (his)) lectures are always fascinating.
Complex sentence	I never miss a class with Professor Chang, **whose** lectures are always fascinating.
Simple sentences	I particularly enjoyed the (last lecture.) (Its) topic was "A Child's First Words."
Complex sentence	I particularly enjoyed the last lecture, **whose** topic was "A Child's First Words."

■ **EXERCISE D**   The sentences on the next page include adjective clauses with *whose*. Rephrase these sentences to form two complete sentences by eliminating *whose* and adding a possessive (or a phrase with *of*).

Example   I have a friend whose wife learned three languages as a child.
I have a friend. His wife learned three languages as a child.

1. Learning a second language seems to be easy for children, whose personalities and brains are still developing.
2. On the other hand, it is more difficult for adults, whose attitudes, habits, and even facial muscles are less flexible.
3. Many people whose minds are open to new experiences enjoy learning new languages at any time.
4. People whose parents and relatives spoke different languages may also find it easier to learn new languages.
5. Languages whose rules and sounds are similar to those of one's native language will be the easiest to learn.

■ **YOUR TURN**   Are people in your culture commonly bilingual or trilingual? What languages do they speak? If two or more languages are spoken at home, when is each language used? For example, do people argue in one language but tell stories in another? Do people use one language among adults and another with children? If you have any experience with bilingualism or trilingualism, share this with your classmates.

■ **EXERCISE E   Review of Adjective Clauses**   Complete the sentences on the next page with *that, which, who,* or *whose,* or use *X* to indicate that no change is necessary. In some cases, more than one relative pronoun may be used. In other cases, the relative pronoun may be omitted. In these cases, give all possibilities but indicate the preferred form.

Examples   Several researchers have tried to teach language to chimpanzees and gorillas, _who_____ are very intelligent members of the monkey family.

The language _that, which, or x_ the researchers taught the chimpanzees was not spoken language, however.

1. Even though they are very intelligent, chimpanzees do not have the vocal apparatus _____ is necessary for producing spoken language.

2. In 1975, two researchers, Beatrice and Allen Gardner, decided to try to teach sign language to a chimpanzee _____ name was Washoe.

3. Sign language, _____ is commonly used by deaf people, involves the use of hand gestures instead of spoken words.

4. After four years of training, Washoe could use 160 signs _____ the Gardners had taught her.

5. The Gardners believed that Washoe, _____ was five years old at the time, resembled a three-year-old child in her communicative ability.

6. Like human children, Washoe used her language to refer to things _____ were not present, such as juice in the refrigerator.

7. Moreover, like human children, she was able to form two-word sentences _____ she had never seen before, such as "More tickle" and "Apple red."

8. The Gardners' experiment, _____ was the first of its kind, was later followed by the work of other experimenters.

9. Scientists _____ have worked closely with chimpanzees for many years believe that chimps have the ability to learn and use basic language for communication.

10. On the other hand, no chimp has ever been able to acquire a large vocabulary or learn complicated grammar rules, _____ all normal children do with little effort.

PART THREE

Adjective Clauses with *Who(m)* and *Which*—Replacement of Objects

TENSION, PRESSURE, PAIN . . . ARE YOU UNDER STRESS?

Do you get angry and impatient when you are forced to wait in traffic or stand in line in a bank? If this happens frequently, you may be suffering from stress. Stress is the uncomfortable feeling that people get in situations that they cannot control.

ADJECTIVE CLAUSES WITH *WHOM* AND *WHICH*— REPLACEMENT OF OBJECTS OF VERBS

The relative pronouns *who(m)* and *which* can replace the object of a verb. *Whom* is used to refer to people only. It is used in formal speaking and writing; *who* is often substituted in informal English. *Which* is used to refer to things or ideas. *Which* must be used in nonrestrictive clauses (with commas). *That* is preferred in restrictive clauses (without commas) that describe things or ideas.

Simple sentences	Dr. Gill will teach a class on the relationship between stress and illness.
	I met Dr. Gill last week.
Complex sentence	Dr. Gill, **whom** I met last week, will teach a course on the relationship between stress and illness.
Simple sentences	Psychology 410 covers methods of reducing stress.
	Dr. Gill teaches Psychology 410.
Complex sentence	Psychology 410, **which** Dr. Gill teaches, covers methods of reducing stress.

■ **EXERCISE A** Underline the adjective clauses in these sentences. Then decide whether the clauses are restrictive or nonrestrictive. Add commas where necessary.

Example Psychosomatic symptoms are physical problems <u>that people get because of stress.</u> *restrictive, no commas*

1. Some psychosomatic symptoms which many people experience are headaches, stomach problems, fatigue, muscle tension, and breathing difficulties.
2. The pain and discomfort which people feel are real, not imaginary.
3. Ulcers which many students develop are a psychosomatic response to the pressures of school and studying.
4. Dr. Gill whom I met at a science convention is teaching a course at the medical school this year.
5. The students whom Dr. Gill spoke to participated in an experiment on stress and high blood pressure.
6. The university which Dr. Gill attended has an excellent psychology department.
7. Stanford University which Dr. Gill attended has an excellent psychology department.
8. Methods of Reducing Stress is a course which all students are required to take.

■ **EXERCISE B** Combine the following sentences by using *whom* or *which*. Form an adjective clause from the second sentence of each pair. Change words and add commas when necessary.

Example Frustration is a feeling. People have it when they cannot reach a goal.
Frustration is a feeling which people have when they cannot reach a goal.

1. According to a 1974 study by two doctors, people with heart disease often showed a certain kind of behavior. The doctors called this behavior "Type A."
2. Patients tended to be angry, hostile, aggressive, very competitive, and easily frustrated. The doctors identified the patients as Type A's.
3. Other patients were easygoing, calm, and relaxed. The doctors labeled them as "Type B's."
4. The Type A's had two to three times as many heart attacks as Type B's. The doctors treated both the Type A's and the Type B's.
5. In treatment, Type A patients learned to act like Type B patients in stressful situations. Many patients claimed the treatment saved their lives.
6. My father is a typical Type A person. I resemble my father in many ways.

■ **YOUR TURN** How would you categorize yourself? What kind of person are you—a Type A or a Type B?

ADJECTIVE CLAUSES WITH *WHOM* AND *WHICH*— REPLACEMENT OF OBJECTS OF PREPOSITIONS

Relative pronouns may replace the object of a preposition. Several constructions are possible, depending on how formal or informal the statement should be. In formal English, the preposition begins the adjective clause. In informal English, the preposition usually follows the verb in the adjective clause. If the preposition begins the clause, *whom, which,* or *whose* must be used. In restrictive clauses with the preposition at the end, the relative pronoun may be dropped.

Simple sentences	**Dr. Church** teaches a course in stress management. I was introduced to **Dr. Church** yesterday.
Complex sentences	Dr. Church, **to whom** I was introduced yesterday, teaches a course in stress management. (formal) Dr. Church, **who(m)** I was introduced **to** yesterday, teaches a course in stress management. (informal)
Simple sentences	**Bascom Hall** is the building. The course is taught in **Bascom Hall**.
Complex sentences	Bascom Hall is the building **in which** the course is taught. (formal) Bascom Hall is the building **which** the course is taught **in**. (informal) Bascom Hall is the building **that** the course is taught **in** (*or* **where** the course is taught). (informal) Bascom Hall is the building **the course is taught in**. (*Note:* This construction is possible with restrictive clauses with the preposition at the end only.)

■ **EXERCISE C** Combine the following sentences by using *whom, that,* or *which* with prepositions. Form adjective clauses from the second sentence in each pair. Give all possible formal and informal patterns. Change words and add commas when necessary.

Example   Anxiety is a state. Everyone suffers from it.

Anxiety is a state
$\begin{cases}\text{from which everyone suffers.} \\ \text{which everyone suffers from.} \\ \text{that everyone suffers from.} \\ \text{everyone suffers from.}\end{cases}$

1. One source of anxiety is a lack of time. Many people complain about a lack of time.
2. People say that there are too many things. They must cope with these things each day.
3. Dr. Church is doing some interesting research on frustration and anxiety. I am studying with her this quarter.
4. Dr. Church has published three important psychology books. I have learned a great deal from these books.
5. Yesterday's lecture was about Dr. Church's latest research on Type A behavior. The students listened to it attentively.
6. One student asked Dr. Church a difficult question. She responded to the question in great detail.

■ **EXERCISE D   Review of Adjective Clauses**   Complete the following sentences by adding *that*, *which*, or *whose*, or use *X* to indicate that no change is needed. Give all possibilities but indicate the preferred form. Add commas where necessary.

1. Nancy suffers from tension headaches, *which*_____ her doctor

   thinks are caused by muscle tension in her forehead.

2. To control her headaches, Nancy is learning to use biofeedback

   _____ does not involve pills or drugs.

3. Biofeedback is a technique _____ many people use to relax

   their muscles and to control pain.

4. Metal discs are placed on Nancy's forehead and connected to a machine _____ measures changes in her level of tension.

5. When Nancy's tension level is high, the machine makes a high-pitched noise. In contrast, when Nancy relaxes, the machine

   _____ senses tiny changes in her body makes a low tone.

6. Nancy uses relaxing thoughts and images to make the machine produce a low tone _____ means the muscles in her forehead are relaxed.

7. The images _____ Nancy uses to produce the low tone are relaxing and peaceful.

8. After several weeks of training, Nancy _____ headaches used to be very painful has learned to decrease her muscle tension. Her headaches have stopped.

■ **EXERCISE E   Review of Adjective Clauses**   Combine the following sentences by using *that, when, where, which, who, whom,* or *whose.* Form adjective clauses from the second sentence in each pair. Use each connecting word at least once. Omit or change words and add commas when necessary.

Example   Two clinical psychologists developed a stress management program for people. The people's lives were filled with stress.
Two clinical psychologists developed a stress management program for people whose lives were filled with stress.

1. The first part of this program involves keeping a diary. You write about your daily problems, feelings, and complaints in the diary.
2. If your diary contains many negative feelings and thoughts, you must learn to replace them with other thoughts. These thoughts are positive.
3. You can also try using relaxation techniques. These techniques work effectively to reduce stressful feelings.
4. Many people relax through meditation. Meditation involves sitting comfortably, concentrating, and trying to clear your mind of upsetting thoughts.
5. A good time to meditate is right after work or school. Right after work or school, you may be tired and anxious from the day's events.
6. You should meditate in a quiet place. No one will disturb you there.
7. Another relaxation method is progressive relaxation. This method is both easy and convenient.
8. Progressive relaxation is a technique. This technique involves tensing and then relaxing all your muscles, beginning with the toes and continuing up the body.
9. Both of these techniques work very well if you practice them regularly. Researchers have studied these techniques in great detail.
10. Finally, the people can make a difference in how you cope with stress. These people surround you.

11. In general, some people are healthier and less anxious than others. These people's families and friends are helpful and supportive.

12. In other words, you will probably be healthier if you have good friends. You can trust your friends.

■ **YOUR TURN** First, summarize what you have learned in this section about biofeedback, meditation, and progressive relaxation. Complete this sentence: *Biofeedback is a technique in which* _____. Then form similar sentences for the other relaxation techniques.

Share your experiences with these techniques. Have you ever tried any of them? Do you know people who have? Have you tried other techniques for relaxing that have been successful?

P A R T   F O U R

Language Activities

The following speaking and writing activities are designed to help you practice a variety of adjective clauses and phrases.

ADJECTIVE CLAUSES — REPLACEMENT OF SUBJECTS

■ **ACTIVITY A** Test your memory by playing a game with definitions. Divide into two groups. A player from team 1 will begin a definition, and a player from team 2 must finish it. Then a different player from team 2 will begin another definition, and a different player from team 1 must finish it. Score one point for each correct completion. The full sentence must use an adjective clause in order to be counted correct. Here are some words from the chapter to define. Use these and add to them or make your own lists.

Example   An anthropologist is a person **who studies the origin and nature of human beings.**

✓ anthropologist	long sleeper	sociologist
insomniac	psychologist	Type A person
linguist	short sleeper	Type B person

ADJECTIVE CLAUSES — REPLACEMENT OF OBJECTS

■ **ACTIVITY B** Think about the high points and low points of your life. Think about the best and worst, the most interesting, and the most frightening. Tell or write several brief stories about them. Below is some vocabulary to give you ideas. Begin your story with *The* (adjective + noun) *that I have ever* . . .

Examples   **The strangest dream that I have ever** had was when I was about seventeen . . .
or
The most embarrassing situation that I have ever been in was during eighth grade . . .
or
The most interesting teacher whom I have ever known was . . .

ADJECTIVES		NOUNS	
best	funny	dream	person
bizarre	interesting	experience	situation
embarrassing	strange	friend	teacher
exciting	worst	meal	trip
frightening		nightmare	

ALL FORMS OF ADJECTIVE CLAUSES

■ **ACTIVITY C** Interview a classmate about his or her language-learning experience. Then use the information to make a brief oral or written report about him or her. Ask your classmate the following questions.

1. What is your first language?
2. Did your parents or close relatives speak another language when you were a child?
3. Are you bilingual or trilingual?
4. In which language did you learn to read? Is it different from the language you spoke at home?
5. What additional languages have you studied? How many years did you study each one? Can you speak them now?
6. Is it easy for you to learn new languages?
7. Which language(s) would you like to study in the future?

When you write or present your report, try to use adjective clauses. For instance, you can begin by saying, "Rina, whose parents come from Romania, was raised in France. Therefore, she can speak both Romanian and French. However, French is the language in which she was educated, so she doesn't know how to read Romanian."

■ **ACTIVITY D**   Why do we act the way we do? What controls our behavior? Some people believe that our religion (or lack of it) governs most of our actions. Others believe that our native language defines not only our culture but also our entire view of the world. And still others believe that our heredity controls us. What is your opinion?

Write an essay on your view of humans and human behavior. Then in small groups, share your thoughts with your classmates.

■ **ACTIVITY E**   This chapter contains a wide variety of vocabulary. Even after you have completed it, there still may be words that confuse you. Make a short list of new vocabulary. Then in small groups, write your own definitions for these words. Definitions commonly use adjective clauses, so try to include these clauses when possible.

After you have written your own definitions, check them with other groups, with your teacher, or with your dictionary. You may also want to define some of the following words.

PART ONE	PART TWO	PART THREE
consciousness	acquisition	biofeedback
EEG	babbling	frustration
insomnia	bilingualism	high blood
recurring dreams	facial expressions	pressure
subconscious	random	psychosomatic
tranquilizers	sign language	symptoms
		ulcer

Example   **Consciousness is the awareness that you have of your surroundings.**

■ **ACTIVITY F**   How many adjective clauses can you put in one sentence? While this may be very poor writing style, it certainly is a test of your knowledge of adjective clauses!

First read the following attempt by one student. How many clauses do you find? Then try an original one. *But remember that this is only for practice.* We do not recommend using dozens of adjective clauses in your sentences!

There was an old man who lived in Mexico City, which is the capital city of Mexico, which is situated between North and South America, who had a big house that was surrounded by a large garden in which a lot of old trees grew and where sat the old Rolls-Royce, in which the old man had driven

5 through the city until he had an accident in which he hurt his legs and arms, which were then put in casts by a doctor who came from the hospital that had been built by the father of the old man who had the accident, and it is now the best hospital in Mexico, the one in which all the most talented surgeons work, most of whom come from the University of Mexico City,

10 which has a large painting on its front wall that was done by Salvador Dali, who is a Spanish surrealistic painter and who is, unbelievably, related to our old man who had the accident in Mexico City, which is, as mentioned above, the capital city of Mexico.

—Hans Jurgen

Answer: 21 clauses

Living Together on a Small Planet

Noun Clauses and Conditional Sentences

In this chapter, you will study noun clauses and conditional sentences with *if*. In studying noun clauses, you will focus on reported speech and embedded questions, and you will also cover the verbs *hope* and *wish*. In sentences with *hope*, *wish*, and *if*, you will look at the contrast between reality and dreams. Finally, the chapter includes a brief review of many structures covered in your text.

Previewing the Passage

When you think about your world, what do you think about? Your home? Your family? Your city? Your country? Or do you consider the planet earth your world?

Our Planet

Although it's often hard to remember, the world we live in is only a fragment in history and in the universe. And despite our different countries and languages, we are *all* a part of this same small fragment of life.

5   Our earth, this small fragment in space and time, gives us life. If our planet had been different — if the earth had been smaller or colder — our world would not be the same. Life might not have developed, and we might not even exist. Our planet, the whole planet, gives us life. And yet, caught up in our own little worlds of families or cities or countries or languages or cultures, we often forget the larger picture.

10   Sometimes it takes an extraordinary event or point of view to remember that there is a larger picture to our lives. For astronaut Russell Schweikert, this came in 1969 as he looked at the earth from space in the Apollo IX Lunar Module. Said Schweikert, "When you go around it [the earth] in an hour and a half, you begin to recognize that your identity is with that *whole* thing. And that

15   makes a change.

"You look down there, and you can't imagine how many borders and boundaries you cross, again and again and again, and you don't even see them. There you are — hundreds of people killing each other over some imaginary line that you're not even aware of, that you can't see. And from where you see it,

20   the thing [the earth] is a whole, and it's so beautiful. And you wish you could take one [person] in each hand and say, 'Look at it from this perspective. What's important?'

"And you realize that on that small spot, that little blue and white thing, is everything that means anything to you. All of history and music and poetry and

25   art and birth and love: tears, joy, games. All of it on that little spot out there that you can cover with your thumb."

Understanding Vocabulary

1. In the passage, Russell Schweikert uses the word *identity,* which comes from the Latin root *idem,* meaning "same." Can you give other forms of this word?

   noun _____ verb _____ adjective _____

2. Schweikert talks about borders as *imaginary* lines on the earth. He also uses a verb form of the same word. Can you find it? What is the root of these words? What other forms do you know?

Discussing the Passage

1. Why do you think Schweikert called borders "imaginary lines"? Are borders imaginary lines? Why or why not?
2. In lines 12–14, Schweikert said, " . . . your identity is with that *whole* thing," meaning the earth. What did he mean by this?

P A R T   O N E

Noun Clauses and Reported Speech

ON FRIENDSHIP

"Someone once said that a true friend was the best possession, and that's a proverb I believe in. I believe that you have to treat your friends with care and affection just as you would your most valuable possession."

—Edward Sonnenberg

Noun Clauses with *That*

Noun clauses may replace nouns or pronouns as subjects, objects, or complements. These clauses often begin with the subordinating conjunction *that*. In conversational English, *that* is frequently omitted.

Noun or pronoun object	I know **something.**	Noun clauses often follow such verbs as *agree, believe, feel, find, hope, know, mention, notice, realize, regret, remark, say, tell, think, understand,* and *wish.*
Noun clause object	I know **(that) friends are important.**	

■ **EXERCISE A**   Answer the following questions in your own words. Use noun clauses after *learn, realize, know, regret,* and *believe.*

1. What have you learned about people in general during this class?
2. What are the three most important things about other cultures that you have learned during this class?
3. What have you realized about your own culture?
4. What are five new things that you now know about English?
5. Is there anything that you regret about your work in English?
6. What do you believe is the most valuable thing about your experience here?

■ **YOUR TURN**   In small groups, discuss some of your answers to the questions in Exercise A. Then choose one member to give a brief report for the class. In your report, use "reporting clauses" such as *We (all) agree (believe, think) that . . . , Several of us feel that . . . , Some of us have found that . . . ,* and so on.

Quotations and Reported Speech

Quotations are the exact words that someone says. They are used with quotation marks. A comma often precedes or follows a quotation. For example,

Ralph Waldo Emerson once said, "The only way to have a friend is to be one."

Reported speech gives the ideas, but *not necessarily* the exact words, of the original speaker. Reported speech does not generally require commas or quotation marks. For example,

Ralph Waldo Emerson once said that the only way to have a friend is/was to be a friend to someone.

Sequence of Tenses in Reported Speech

Verbs and certain modal auxiliaries may shift to past forms in reported speech. These shifts most often occur when the report is being given at a different time or place than the action. If the information is still true at the moment of speaking, the shift from present to past may be optional. The changes must be consistent, however. *That* is also optional in most of these sentences.

$\longrightarrow$

	QUOTATION	REPORTED SPEECH	NOTES
Changes in tenses	"Max is at home."	Molly said Max was at home.	In reported speech, when the verb in the main clause (*Molly said, She mentioned*, etc.) is in the past, the verb in the noun clause is often in a past tense. The verb in the noun clause may shift from present to past or present perfect to past perfect.
	"Max is studying."	She mentioned that he was studying.	
	"He is going to study all day."	She remarked that he was going to study all day.	
	"He has a lot of work."	She said he had a lot of work.	
	"He hasn't fin- ished yet."	She added he hadn't finished yet.	
	"He began Monday."	She said he began (had begun) Monday.	The shift of simple past and past continuous tenses in the noun clause to perfect forms is often optional.*
	"He was working very hard."	She said he was working (had been working) very hard.	
Changes in modal auxiliaries†	"Max can't go."	She said that Max couldn't go.	*Can* often shifts to *could.*
	"Sam may go."	She remarked that Sam might go.	*May* often shifts to *might.*
	"He will tell us."	She added he would tell us.	*Will* often shifts to *would.*
	"He must finish his work."	She stressed that he had to finish his work.	*Must* is sometimes changed to *had to* when need is expressed.

$\longrightarrow$

---

* In some cases, use of the past perfect or past perfect continuous changes the meaning. It can indicate that a situation is finished or is no longer true. Compare: *He said that he wanted to go.* (Perhaps he still wants to.) *He said that he had wanted to go.* (He no longer wants to or he can't go.)

† In reported speech, modals are changed less frequently than other verbs or auxiliaries because of the problems of differences in meaning.

	QUOTATION	REPORTED SPEECH	NOTES
Changes in commands	"Let's leave at 8:00."	She said that we should leave at 8:00.	An appropriate noun or pronoun is added in reported speech. *Should* or other modal auxiliaries are used, depending on the strength of the original command.
	"Be on time."	She told me very firmly that I must be on time.	

■ **EXERCISE B** Even good friends have problems, and one way to save friendships is by talking things over. In the following conversation, a group of roommates is trying to resolve a common problem, housework. Retell the conversation in reported speech by completing the sentences below. Be sure to use appropriate verb forms in your new sentences.

Example   Steve said that they *should talk things over*   .

STEVE: We're all good friends, but we've been having a lot of problems lately.

TOM: Well, in my opinion, the biggest problem is cleaning. The apartment is a mess. Nobody cleaned last week or the week before. We must find a way to keep things cleaner.

JOHN: We can make a list of jobs to do, and each person can sign up for a job.

PETER: I'll be responsible for the kitchen area.

TOM: I'll do the living room, but we need a vacuum cleaner!

STEVE: I'm going to check the newspaper. I may be able to find a good used one.

1. Steve remarked that they _____ but that they _____.

2. Tom felt the biggest problem _____ and the apartment _____.

3. He added that nobody _____ and that they _____.

4. John remarked that they _____ and that each person _____.

5. Peter stated that he _____.

6. Tom added that he _____ but that they _____.

7. Steve mentioned that he _____.

8. He added that he _____.

■ **EXERCISE C** Reread the conversation in Exercise B. Then complete the following with the past form of *say* or *tell*.

1. Steve *said*_____ that they'd been having a lot of problems lately.

2. Tom _____ his roommates that cleaning was their biggest problem.

3. John _____ that they could each choose a job to do.

4. Peter _____ that he would clean the kitchen.

5. Tom _____ everyone that he would take care of the living room.

6. Finally, Steve _____ the others that he would try to find a vacuum cleaner.

Say Versus *Tell*

Molly **said** that Max had to work.	In general, *say* is used when the listener is *not* mentioned.
Molly **told me** that Max had to work.	*Tell* is used when the listener *is* mentioned. (We say something, but we tell *someone* something.)

Pronoun and Adverb Changes in Reported Speech

In reported speech, pronouns are changed to show a change in speakers. Adjectives and adverbs are sometimes changed too. The use of *this, that, these, those, now, then, here,* and *there* depends on the time and place of the reported speech. *Today, tomorrow,* and *yesterday* may also change according to the time of the reported speech. Remember to be consistent. If you make the change in one place, you must make it in all cases.

Pronouns	Mary said, "I need your help."	Mary said that she needed my help.
	Mary said, "We must finish soon!"	Mary said we had to finish soon.
	Erik said, "You have to finish immediately."	Erik said that we had to finish immediately.
Demonstrative pronouns and adjectives	Mary said, "This is important."	Mary said that was important.
	Mary said, "These papers are important."	Mary said those papers were important.
Adverbs	Mary said, "I need them now."	Mary said she needed them then.
	Mary said, "The papers are here."	Mary said that the papers were there.

■ **EXERCISE D** The following quotations are students' responses to various questions. Change each quotation to reported speech. Make all necessary changes in verb tenses, pronouns, and so on. Note that you do not need to use a "reporting clause" with every sentence; however, you do need to be consistent in all changes.

Example   "I've really learned a lot here. I even learned how to surf!"
—Noriko, female, Japan
Noriko said that she had really learned a lot there. She'd even learned how to surf.

1. What has been the best part of your stay in California?
   a. "I've made wonderful new friends during my visit. I hope some of them will come to see me in Japan."
   —Masahiko, male, Japan
   b. "I got married."—Walter, male, Poland
2. What do you like best about Boston?
   a. "I really enjoy the incredible variety of people here."
   —Odelmo, male, Venezuela
   b. "I can do almost anything here. This afternoon I may see a movie; there are at least ten good ones to pick from. Or I may go to a museum; there are several excellent ones."
   —Frank, male, Switzerland
3. How did you like the experience of spending a winter in Wisconsin?
   a. "We were extremely cold at first! We weren't used to cold weather at all. Little by little, my family is learning to adapt to it."
   —Lijia, female, Nicaragua
   b. "It was difficult at the beginning. Some days I almost froze while I was walking home. I'm finally getting used to it."
   —Bedi, male, Mauritania

■ **YOUR TURN** In pairs or small groups, ask each other questions similar to those in Exercise D. Then briefly tell the whole group what your classmates said. Use (*Name of classmate*) *said / told me* in your report.

Verbs and Modal Auxiliaries That Do Not Change in Reported Speech

	QUOTATIONS	REPORTED SPEECH	NOTES
No tense changes	Molly says, "Max is at home." Molly adds, "He hasn't finished his work yet."	Molly says Max is at home. Molly adds that he hasn't finished his work yet.	In reported speech, no tense change occurs when the verb in the main clause is in the present tense.

→

	QUOTATIONS	REPORTED SPEECH	NOTES
Optional tense changes	Molly said, "Max is a hard worker."	Molly said Max was (is) a hard worker.	When the noun clause gives factual information that is true in general, either present or past forms may be used.
	Molly said, "He works very hard."	Molly said he worked (works) very hard.	
No change in modal auxiliaries	Molly said, "Max should finish soon."	Molly said Max should finish soon.	*Could, might, ought to, should,* and *would* are not generally changed in reported speech.
	Molly added, "He must be tired."	Molly added that he must be tired.	*Must* does not change when it expresses probability.
	She remarked, "He ought to have started sooner."	She remarked that he ought to have started sooner.	Perfect modals are not changed in reported speech.

■ **EXERCISE E Error Analysis** Many of the following statements have errors in their use of reported speech. Note that most of these statements can be true at any time, so certain changes will be optional. As you find the various errors, remember to be consistent in your corrections.

Example Ralph Waldo Emerson ~~says~~ *said* that the only way to have a friend <u>was</u> to be one. *Either <u>was</u> or <u>is</u> is correct.*

1. Charles Colton once wrote that true friendship was like good health. The value of it is seldom known until it is lost.

2. Elbert Hubbard remarked that your friend is the person who knows all about me and still liked me.

3. In her book *Emma*, Jane Austen wrote that business might bring money, but friendship hardly ever did.

4. Ned Rorem once commented that sooner or later you've heard all my best friends have to say. Now came the tolerance of real love.

5. In his journals, Emerson remarked that one of the blessings of old friends was that you can afford to be stupid with them.

6. Kurt Vonnegut wrote that love was where you find it. It was foolish to go looking for it.

7. In the first century, a Roman author comments that the friendship that can come to an end had never really begun.

8. La Rochefoucauld wrote in his *Maxims* that however rare true love may be, it is less rare than true friendship.

■ **YOUR TURN**   Share your own thoughts with your classmates. Do you agree with the statements from Exercise E? Can you think of other sayings about love or friendship from your culture?

■ **EXERCISE F**   Answer the following questions in your own words, using reported speech where appropriate.

1. When did you last talk to your best friend or another friend whom you hadn't seen for a while? What did you talk about? What news did your friend tell you? What did you say about that? What news did you tell your friend?

2. Have you made a promise lately? To whom did you make the promise? What did you promise?

3. Have you had an argument lately? What was it about? Whom did you argue with? What did you say to each other? How did you settle the argument?

4. Have you had to make a decision or solve a problem lately? What was the situation? Did you discuss it with anyone? What did you talk about? What advice did the person give you?

P A R T   T W O

Noun Clauses and Embedded Questions — Clause-to-Phrase Reduction

EDUCATION FOR A SMALL PLANET

"It is not a question of how much a man knows, but what use he makes of what he knows. Not a question of what he has acquired and how he has been trained, but of what he is and what he can do."

—J. G. Holland

Noun Clauses with *If* and *Whether*

YES/NO QUESTIONS	NOUN CLAUSES WITH *IF* AND *WHETHER*	NOTES
Is he going?	I wonder **if** he is going.	Yes/no questions may be changed into noun clauses by using *if* and *whether*. The subject must come *before* the verb in the noun clause. Noun clauses with *if* and *whether* are often used in polite requests such as *I would like to know . . .* or *Could you tell me . . . ?*
Has he left yet?	Do you know **whether** he has left yet?	
Can he go?	I wonder **whether** he can go.	
Does he want to go?	Could you tell me **if** he wants to go?	
Did he leave?	I would like to know **whether** he left.	

■ **EXERCISE A** You are in the final chapter of this book. Do you have an assignment or test in the next few days? Take this opportunity to ask your teacher for more information about the final days of this session. Change the following direct questions to noun clauses. Be sure to use correct word order. Begin your questions with the following: *Could you tell me . . . ? I would like to know . . .*

Example   Will there be any more homework this session?
I would like to know whether (if) there will be any more homework this quarter.

1. Will there be a final test in this class?
2. Do I have to take a proficiency exam?
3. Is it necessary to study for the proficiency test?
4. Have I completed all of the assignments for this class?
5. Am I going to pass this course?
6. Could I talk to you about my progress?
7. Will we have a class party?
8. Does anyone want to plan a party?

Noun Clauses with Question Words

INFORMATION QUESTIONS	NOUN CLAUSES WITH QUESTION WORDS	NOTES
Where is the library?	I would like to know **where the library is**.	Information questions may also be changed to noun clauses. Question words such as *When, Where,* and *How* are used to introduce them. The subject must come *before* the verb in noun clauses. These clauses are often used in polite requests, such as *I would like to know . . . , Could you tell me . . . ,* and so on.
How can I find it?	Please tell me **how I can find it**.	
When does it close?	Do you know **when it closes**?	

■ **EXERCISE B**   Imagine that you have to write a term paper for a class. Change the following questions about the assignment to noun clauses. Be sure to use correct word order. Begin your new sentences with the following.

- Could you tell me . . . ?
- I would like to know . . .
- I wonder . . .
- I don't know . . .

Example   When is the paper due?
             Could you tell me when the paper is due?

1. How long should the paper be?
2. How many sources should I use?
3. Where can I get information on the topic?
4. Which section of the library should I check?
5. When could I discuss this with you?
6. Where can I find someone to type it?

■ **EXERCISE C**   The following is an excerpt from an interview with Meredith Pike, an educational consultant to the San Francisco public schools. The interviewer is Martha Brown.

First read the interview for meaning. Then paraphrase the discussion by completing the sentences below. Remember to use reported speech and try to simplify ideas whenever possible.

MARTHA BROWN: What is the greatest problem facing the public schools?

MEREDITH PIKE: The greatest problem is class size. The average public school class has twenty-eight students. When class size is too big, teachers can't help students individually.

BROWN: What's the solution?

PIKE: The solution is to develop strategies that help students learn in large groups. Cooperative learning is one of these strategies.

BROWN: What does it involve?

PIKE: Cooperative learning involves dividing the class into smaller groups. Teachers' jobs become easier because they deal with the groups instead of individuals. The students learn more because each one in the group has a responsibility—for example, the stronger students help the weaker ones. The students learn the material and, at the same time, learn cooperation, an important life skill.

BROWN: How realistic is this solution?

PIKE: It's very realistic, but it takes time and commitment because teachers and administrators have to be trained in new methods.

Example Martha Brown began by asking what . . .
Martha Brown began by asking what the greatest problem facing the public schools was.

 1. Pike stated . . .
 2. She explained that the average public school . . . and that . . .
 3. Next, Brown asked . . .
 4. Pike answered that . . .
 5. She said that cooperative learning . . .
 6. Brown then asked . . .
 7. Pike responded that . . .
 8. She stated that teachers' jobs . . . and that the students . . .
 9. She added that the students . . .
10. Finally, Brown asked . . .
11. Pike said . . . but . . . because . . .

■ **EXERCISE D** **Review** Individually, in pairs, or in small groups, combine the following pairs or groups of sentences. Many variations are possible; above all, try to vary your sentence structures and to eliminate unnecessary words.

HOW CAN PEOPLE LEARN BEST?

Example The greatest puzzle of education is a question.
How can a child learn best?

1. People everywhere agree on an idea.
   Education is important.
   Few people agree on something.
   How should we provide education?

2. Does a child learn well in these ways?
   Information is taught by practice.
   Information is taught by repetition.
   Information is taught by memorization.

3. Does a child learn better in other ways?
   The teacher stimulates the child's curiosity.
   The teacher makes learning fun.
   The teacher makes learning pleasant.

4. Are there certain subjects?
   These subjects must be memorized.
   These include the alphabet and numbers.
   These include the rules of spelling.
   These include the multiplication tables.

5. Memorization is a part of education.
   Repetitive drill is a part of education.

6. Does this mean something?
   Can most learning be taught in that way?
   Should most learning be taught in that way?

7. Should learning be fun for the student?
   Is schooling very hard work?
   The student must be forced to do it.

■ **YOUR TURN** In pairs or in small groups, discuss the questions raised in Exercise D. What are your opinions on the best ways to study and learn? After you have finished your discussion, choose one member to give a brief summary for the entire class. Be sure to use reported speech in your summary.

PART   THREE

Hope, Wish, and Conditional Sentences — Present and Future Time

WHAT TO DO?

"Being a teenager in today's world isn't easy. Sometimes I wish that I lived in a different place or that I had been born in a simpler time. There are just so many choices today. If I knew the right thing to do, I'd do it. But most of the time, I'm just not sure."

—Susan Fox, age 17

HOPE VERSUS *WISH*

The verb *hope* is generally used to express optimism; the speaker feels that something is possible. The verb *wish* is often used to express impossibility or improbability; the speaker wants reality to be different than it is. To show the contrast to reality, *would, could,* or a special verb form — the subjunctive mood — is used after *wish*. The subjunctive mood shows that the ideas are imaginary, improbable, or contrary to fact.

HOPES AND WISHES	MEANING
I **hope** that he **will go.** I **hope** he **is going.**	I think that he may go (and I want him to go).
I **wish** that he **would go.** I **wish** he **were going**.	I don't think he's going to go (but I would like him to go).

→

wishes about the present

I **wish** that they **were** here. (They aren't here.)

I **wish** they **were coming**. (I think they aren't coming.)

I **wish** that they **came** more often. (They don't come very often.)

wishes about the future

I **wish** he **would (could) go.**

I **wish** he **were going to go.** (I think that he isn't going to come.)

wishes about the past

I **wish** she **had come.** (She didn't come.)

I **wish** she **had been** here. (She wasn't here.)

Present and future wishes are expressed by using *would, could,* or **a** subjunctive verb form. In most cases, this form is the same as the simple past tense. However, in formal English, *were* is used for all forms of the verb *be.* In informal English, *was* is often used with *I, he, she,* and *it.*

Past wishes are also expressed by using a subjunctive verb form. This form is the same as the past perfect tense in all cases, *had* + past participle.

■ **EXERCISE A**   Underline the verbs in the dependent clauses. Do the verbs refer to the present, past, or future? Indicate the time frame of each. Then rephrase each sentence to show its meaning.

Examples
future
I wish I <u>were going to go</u> to Spain. **I'm probably not going to go to Spain, but I would like to.**

present
I wish that you <u>were</u> here. **You're not here, and I miss you.**

past
I wish that I <u>had gone</u> with you. **I didn't go with you. I feel unhappy about that.**

1. I wish that I were going to study in Europe next year.

2. I wish that I hadn't quit my job in the summer.

3. I wish that I had more money.

4. I wish that traveling were cheaper.

5. I wish that I had studied harder before final exams.

6. I wish that I could forget all my problems.

■ **EXERCISE B** Many North Americans, especially young people, put bumper stickers on their cars that tell you what they would rather be doing. It's a way of forgetting about the present and wishing things were different. Rephrase the following sentences to use *wish*.

Example   I'd rather be skiing.
              I wish I were skiing.

1. I'd rather be sailing.
2. We'd rather be jogging.
3. I'd rather be in Paris.
4. I'd rather not be driving.
5. I'd rather be windsurfing.
6. We'd rather be playing tennis.
7. I'd rather be in Rio.
8. I'd rather not be going to work.

■ **YOUR TURN** Right now you are studying English. As you are reading this, what do you wish you were doing (or *not* doing)? Give at least six sentences.

Example   **I wish I were swimming. I wish I didn't have to do this work. I wish I could go to the beach.**

■ **EXERCISE C** In groups of three, take turns making statements and responses.

Example   My brother left home last year.
              STUDENT A: **My brother left home last year.**
              STUDENT B: **Don't you wish you had left home last year too?**
              STUDENT C: **Of course.**
                          or
                          Not really.

1. My brother went to Japan last year.
2. He got a scholarship at the university.
3. He learned to speak Japanese fluently.
4. He got a degree in business.
5. He received an award for academic excellence.
6. Then he won the lottery!

■ **EXERCISE D**   Complete the following passage with the appropriate forms of the verbs in parentheses. Be sure to add modal auxiliaries when necessary.

CITY LIVING

My name's Mario. I live in a big city. It's a beautiful city in a lot of ways, but our neighborhood is pretty tough. I wish things _were_____ (be) a lot different. For example, I live a long way from school. I wish that I _____$_1$ (not have) to get up at 6:00 A.M. to take a bus to school. I wish my school _____$_2$ (be) right next door. And I wish the whole neighborhood _____$_3$ nicer and cleaner. I wish people _____$_4$ (clean) up around here—and not just the garbage! I wish there _____$_5$ (not be) any drugs on the streets. I wish I _____$_6$ (go) out alone at night. Sometimes I wish that my parents _____$_7$ (never move) here. I hope things _____$_8$ (change). I hope I _____$_9$ (go) to college and help my family.

Imaginative Conditional Sentences—Present or Unspecified Time

Imaginative conditional sentences express conditions that the speaker or writer thinks are unlikely, untrue, or contrary to fact. They may be wishes and dreams, or they may express advice to others.

In these sentences, the subjunctive is used in the *if* clause. In most cases, this form is the same as the simple past tense. For the verb *be*, however, *were* is used for all persons in formal English.

CONDITIONAL SENTENCE	MEANING
If I **had** more money, I **might take** some trips.	I don't have much money, so I don't take many trips.
I **could travel** around the world if I **were** rich.	I can't travel around the world because I don't have the money.
If I **were** you, I **would try** to save more money.	My advice is that you should try to save more money.

■ **EXERCISE E**   Complete the following in your own words. Try to give several sentences for each.

Example   I don't have a job, but if I did, **I wouldn't have any free time.**
I would have more money to spend.

1. I don't have much money, but if I did, . . .
2. I don't have much free time, but if I did, . . .
3. I'm not a good cook, but if I were, . . .
4. I don't have a car, but if I did, . . .
5. I don't have a husband (wife), but if I did, . . .

■ **YOUR TURN**   Add two or three original sentences. You might want to talk about health, family, or job issues.

Example   **I don't have children, but if I did, I would have to move to a bigger apartment.**

■ **EXERCISE F**   Add to the following statements by making a sentence beginning with *If*.

Example   I wish I had more free time. If . . .

I wish I had more free time. If I had more free time, I could (would) travel more.

1. I wish I were at home. If . . .
2. I wish I were younger (older). If . . .
3. I wish I spoke English better. If . . .
4. I wish there were only one language. If . . .
5. I wish our teachers didn't give so much homework. If . . .

■ **YOUR TURN**   Are you talkative? shy? impatient? patient? Are you a good listener? Do you have a good memory? What are some characteristics or traits you wish you had? Give several original sentences using *If I were* or *If I weren't*.

Example   **If I weren't so careless, I would do better on tests.**

■ **EXERCISE G**   In pairs or in small groups, take turns explaining a problem or situation and giving advice on how to deal with it.

Examples   I get frequent headaches, and sometimes I can't see clearly.
If I were you, I would go to an eye doctor.
If I were you, I would have my eyes checked.

Here are some problems you may have had. Feel free to include your own.

1. I'm always late.
2. My roommates are very noisy.
3. I speak my own language more than I speak English.
4. I need a much higher score on the TOEFL to get into the school that I am interested in.
5. The car that I have now uses a lot of gas.
6. I never seem to have any money left at the end of the month.

■ **EXERCISE H**   Answer the following questions in your own words.

1. If you had the chance to go anywhere you wanted, where might you go?
2. If you were able to go back in time, which year or era would you choose? Why would you choose that time?
3. If you had the opportunity to talk with a special person again, who would it be? Why?
4. If you were president of your country, what changes would you make there?
5. If you could do one thing to make the world better, what would it be?

PART FOUR

Perfect Modal Auxiliaries and Conditional Sentences — Past and Past-to-Present Time

THERE'S STILL TIME

"OK, it's true. If we humans had been a little smarter, if we had done more planning, our world would be a much better place. We wouldn't have created giant cities without efficient transportation systems. We wouldn't have polluted our air, land, and water.

"Is it too late? Absolutely not! We got ourselves into this mess; we can certainly get ourselves out."

—Jack Powers
age fortyish

PERFECT MODAL AUXILIARIES

Perfect modal auxiliaries express past activities or situations that were not real or that did not occur. Often they express our wishes in hindsight.

UNFULFILLED INTENTIONS AND PREFERENCES

would	I **would have gone,** but it was impossible.	*Would have* refers to past intentions that were not fulfilled.

UNFULFILLED ADVICE

should	You **should have gone** too. You **shouldn't have stayed** here.	*Should have* and *ought to have* refer to actions that were advisable but did not take place.
ought to	He **ought to have stayed** longer.	*Ought to have* is less common than *should have*.

PAST POSSIBILITIES

could might may	I **could have gone** later. He **might have called.** He **may have left** already.	*Could have, may have,* and *might have* refer to past possibilities. In many cases, the speaker or writer is uncertain whether the action took place. In some contexts, *could have* also refers to past abilities.

■ **EXERCISE A Oral Practice** Change the modals to perfect forms in the following sentences. Then listen carefully as your teacher reads both the present and past forms rapidly. Try to distinguish between the two. What clues can you find to help you distinguish the two forms in rapid speech?

Example   He may leave.
　　　　　　He may have left.

1. I might go.
2. She could forget about it.
3. He would help us.
4. They should call us.
5. She would rather stay home.
6. He should study more.
7. We ought to finish early.
8. You shouldn't let her do that.
9. It wouldn't cost a lot.
10. She might come with us.
11. He may quit his job.

■ **EXERCISE B** We often use responses with modal auxiliaries as a way of empathizing, saying that we understand what someone else feels. In pairs, take turns making statements and responses.

Example   I was excited about going to Los Angeles.
STUDENT A: **I was excited about going to Los Angeles.**
STUDENT B: **I would have been excited too.**

1. I was nervous about the plane trip.
2. I enjoyed the warm weather.
3. I was surprised at the amount of pollution.
4. My eyes hurt from the smog.
5. I got lost on the freeways.

■ **YOUR TURN** Have you felt nervous, excited, worried, or angry about something lately? Share your thoughts with a partner about an experience that was difficult or exciting. Your partner should express understanding using perfect modals in the responses.

Example   STUDENT A: **I was nervous about the test.**
STUDENT B: **I would have been nervous too.**

■ **EXERCISE C** Think about the serious environmental issues we face today—air and water pollution and problems with garbage and hazardous waste disposal, to name a few. What *might, could,* or *should* our governments *have done* in the past to avoid these? Form a complete sentence from each cue. Then give at least one original idea for each problem.

Example   promote energy-efficient homes, factories, and offices
The government could have promoted energy-efficient homes, factories, and offices.

1. Energy production and consumption
   a. begin conservation efforts long ago
   b. require more fuel-efficient automobiles
   c. _____

2. Air pollution
   a. develop good mass transportation systems
   b. promote cars that do not use gasoline
   c. _____

3. Clean water
   a. give serious penalties to polluting industries
   b. control the use of dangerous chemicals
   c. _____

4. Waste disposal

    a. ban the use of certain types of containers

    b. begin recycling programs long ago

    c. _____

■ **YOUR TURN**   What *can* or *should* we do about these problems *today*? Try to give at least one practical idea for each problem mentioned above.

Imaginative Conditional Sentences — Past Time

Conditional sentences with *if* can be used to describe past situations or events that did *not* take place. The subjunctive is used in the *if* clause. In all cases, this form is the same as the past perfect tense. Perfect forms of modal auxiliaries are used in the main clause.

CONDITIONAL SENTENCE	MEANING
If we **had known** about the problem, we **would have done** something about it.	We didn't know about the problem. As a result, we didn't do anything about it.
We **could have helped** if we **had known** about the situation.	We didn't know about the situation, so we weren't able to help.

■ **EXERCISE D**   Imagine that it is now the year 2099. Your home is earth, and it is a very pleasant place. As the twenty-second century approaches, you are looking back and imagining what might have or might not have happened during the twenty-first century. Use past subjunctive forms of the verbs in parentheses or add perfect modal auxiliaries to complete the following passage.

LOOKING BACK AT THE YEARS 2000–2098

Life in the twenty-first century has been very pleasant, thanks to a memorable event in the year 2010. In that year, the entire world decided to work together. The twenty-first century *would (might) have been*   (be) very different if that event _____ ₁ (happen / never).

If we _____ ₂ (not decide) to work together, there _____ ₃ (be) a total disaster. Our environment _____ ₄ (damage) beyond repair if we _____ ₅ (not control) pollution, use of resources, and farming and fishing methods. The population of the world _____ ₆ (continue) to grow, and more and more people _____ ₇ (move) to the cities.

If the earth's population _____ ₈ (continue) to grow, we _____ ₉ (not provide) free medical care and education for everyone. There _____ ₁₀ (be) problems with jobs. And of course, there _____ ₁₁ (not be) enough food to go around.

Fortunately, though, at the beginning of the twenty-first century, our governments were very wise. As a result, we have a healthy environment, sufficient food and medical care, free education, and safe, interesting jobs for everyone. By working together, we have created a very nice place for all the citizens of the earth.

■ **EXERCISE E** Think about how your life might or would have been different if you had made different choices in the past. Answer these questions in your own words. Be sure to explain your reasons for each answer.

1. If you had had the choice, where would you have been born?
2. If you had been able to choose, would you have grown up in a city or in the country? Why?
3. If you had chosen a different language to study, what might it have been?
4. If you had chosen a different city to study in, where would you have gone?
5. If you had chosen a different career, what might you have studied? Why?

Imaginative Conditional Sentences — Past-to-Present Time

Conditional sentences with *if* can be used to describe past actions or situations that have affected the present. The subjunctive is used in the *if* clause. In all cases, this form is the same as the past perfect tense. Present forms of modal auxiliaries are used in the main clause.

CONDITIONAL SENTENCE	MEANING
If we **had been** more careful in the past, we **might not have** so many problems.	We were not careful in the past. As a result, we have quite a few problems.
On the other hand, our lives **would be** much harder today if we **hadn't tried** new ideas.	Our lives are not as hard today because we tried new ideas.

■ **EXERCISE F** Imagine how our lives might be different today if these events had not occurred. Complete the following in your own words. Try to give at least one positive and one negative result for each item.

Example   If internal combustion engines hadn't been developed,
we wouldn't have cars, buses, tractors, or airplanes.
we might not have so many problems with air pollution.

1. If cars hadn't been invented, . . .
2. If petroleum hadn't been discovered, . . .
3. If elevators hadn't been invented, . . .
4. If airplanes hadn't been invented, . . .
5. If scientists hadn't learned how to split the atom, . . .

■ **YOUR TURN** Think of other major advances — in technology, medicine, and so on. Imagine life without telephones, televisions, and computers or life without aspirin or antibiotics. How would our lives be different today if these advances had not occurred? Try to add at least four original sentences.

■ **EXERCISE G** Consider past events in your own life and how they have affected your life today. Complete the following in your own words.

1. If I had never studied English, . . .
2. If I had not come to this school, . . .
3. If I had been born the opposite sex, . . .
4. If I had been born sixty years ago, . . .
5. If I had been elected president of my country ten years ago, . . .

■ **EXERCISE H Verb Tense Review** Complete the following with appropriate active or passive forms of the verbs in parentheses. In some cases, you will need to add modal auxiliaries. Some items may have more than one correct answer.

LIFE ON EARTH

Life on earth _developed_ (develop) because the conditions _____₁ (be) suitable for it. If the earth _____₂ (be) smaller or colder, for example, life _____₃ (have) different forms. If the conditions _____₄ (not be) suitable, no living organisms _____₅ (develop) on earth at all.

The simplest living creatures _____₆ (consist) of a single living unit, the cell. More complex creatures _____₇ (make) up of hundreds and even millions of cells. However, all living organisms _____₈ (share) certain characteristics. These _____₉ (include) reproduction, response, growth, and use of energy. Plants and animals _____₁₀ (be) different only in the way that the basic activities of life _____₁₁ (carry) out by each organism.

Of all the creatures alive on earth, humans _____₁₂ (have) the greatest impact. The impact of humans _____₁₃ (come / often) because we _____₁₄ (be) able to think. The power to think _____₁₅ (give) us ways both to create and to destroy.

In the past, humans _____₁₆ (have) less impact, especially on the environment. Because early humans _____₁₇ (move) from place to place, their movement _____₁₈ (give) nature a chance to recover. For example, even though humans _____ 19 (cut) trees, forests _____ 20 (return / soon) to their former size after the humans _____ 21 (move) on.

Today, nature _____ 22 (give / seldom) a chance to recover. Our demands on the earth _____ 23 (increase) steadily. All human activity _____ 24 (seem) to require more and more land and more and more resources. Humans _____ 25 (share) this earth with millions of other animals and plants, yet we _____ 26 (act / often) without ever thinking about our impact on our world.

■ **EXERCISE I Review** Choose the correct forms of the words in parentheses. An *X* indicates that no word is necessary.

LIVING TOGETHER ON A SMALL PLANET*

The environment is (X / (the)) world (that / who)₁ all living things share. It is what is—air, fire, wind, water, life, and sometimes (the / X)₂ culture. The environment consists of all the things that act and (is / are)₃ acted upon. Living creatures (is / are)₄ born into the environment and (are / were)₅ part of it too. Yet there is (no / none)₆ creature (who / whom)₇ perceives all of what is and what happens. A dog perceives things (that / what)₈ we can't, and we perceive and understand (much / many)₉ things beyond (its / it's)₁₀ world. For a dog, a book isn't much different from a stick, (while / on the other hand)₁₁ for us, one stick is pretty much like every other stick. There is no world (that / who)₁₂ is experienced (by / from)₁₃ all living creatures. (Despite / Although)₁₄ we all live in the same environment, we create many worlds.

We actually know very (little / few)₁₅ of the world, even of what (does surround / surrounds)₁₆ us every day. It is worth (to take / taking)₁₇ the time (to think / thinking)₁₈ of the variety of ways in (that / which)₁₉ the

---

* Adapted from Judith and Herbert Kohl, *The View from the Oak*. Sierra Club Books.

environment could be structured and (to discover / discovering)$_{20}$ how (X / do)$_{21}$ different living things actually structure it. We are all collections of atoms, specks in (X / the)$_{22}$ universe, just the right size in our own worlds, giants to fleas, midgets to whales. Our view of the world is only one of (many / much)$_{23}$. It enriches (our / us)$_{24}$ understanding of ourselves to move away from familiar worlds and attempt to understand the experience of others . . . The respect for life we can (gain / to gain)$_{25}$ from these efforts (might / might have)$_{26}$ in some small way help us work toward (preserving / to preserve)$_{27}$ the world we share.

PART FIVE

Language Activities

The following speaking and writing activities are designed to help you practice the structures covered in this chapter, noun clauses and conditional sentences.

NOUN CLAUSES — REPORTED SPEECH

■ **ACTIVITY A**   In small groups, discuss the following quotations about friendship. After you have finished your discussion, choose a spokesperson to give a brief report to the class. Be sure to use reported speech in the summary of your discussion.

"No man is an island . . . ; every man is . . . , a part of the main. . . . Any man's death diminishes me because I am involved in mankind; and therefore never send to know for whom the bell tolls; it tolls for thee."
　　　　　　　　　　—John Donne, *Devotions upon Emergent Occasions*

"He who has a thousand friends has not a friend to spare,
And he who has one enemy will meet him everywhere."
　　　　　　　　　　—Ali ibn-Abi-Talib, *A Hundred Sayings*

"I wish that people who are conventionally supposed to love each other would say to each other when they fight, 'Please—a little less love, and a little more common decency.'"
　　　　　　　　　　—Kurt Vonnegut, *Slapstick*

NOUN CLAUSES — EMBEDDED QUESTIONS

■ **ACTIVITY B**   Imagine that you have the opportunity to question today's world leaders on their policies. In small groups, prepare a list of three world leaders and of at least ten issues that you would like these leaders to address. Use expressions such as *We would like to know* and *Could you please explain to us* in your questions. Then take turns role-playing world leaders. You may want to organize a panel that will answer questions in a "Face the Nation [the World]" format. The rest of the class will ask the questions.

HOPE VERSUS *WISH*

■ **ACTIVITY C**   A genie has granted you three wishes. Anything that you want will come true. All you have to do is wish. Think about what you would like to happen. Then share your wishes with your classmates. Be sure to explain what would happen if your wishes came true!

CONDITIONAL SENTENCES — PRESENT OR UNSPECIFIED TIME

■ **ACTIVITY D**   John F. Kennedy often spoke about ideals and about making our world a better place. Perhaps because of this, he helped inspire an entire generation of young people. During one such speech at Harvard University in 1953, he said, "If more politicians knew poetry, and more poets knew politics, I am convinced the world would be a better place in which to live."

What do you think Kennedy meant by this? In a discussion or in writing, share your ideas on Kennedy's words.

■ **ACTIVITY E** Hindsight is the knowledge and understanding we have when we look back in time. As you read the following passage, think about second chances, the opportunities to try again. Are there things that you would do differently if you had the chance? Tell or write about your ideas.

IF I HAD MY LIFE TO DO OVER

I'd make a few more mistakes next time. I'd relax. I would limber up. I would be sillier than I had been this trip. I would take fewer things seriously. I would climb more mountains and swim more rivers. I would eat more ice cream and less beans. I would perhaps have more actual trou-

5   bles, but I'd have fewer imaginary ones.

You see, I'm one of those people who live sensibly and sanely hour after hour, day after day. Oh, I've had my moments, and if I had it to do over again, I'd have more of them. In fact, I'd try to have nothing else. Just moments, one after another, instead of living so many years ahead of each

10   day. I've been one of those persons who never goes anywhere without a hot-water bottle and a parachute. If I had it to do again, I would travel lighter.

If I had my life to do over again, I would start barefoot earlier in the spring and stay that way later in the fall. I would go to more dances. I

15   would ride more merry-go-rounds. I would pick more daisies.

—Nadine Stair, age 85, Louisville, Kentucky

CONDITIONAL SENTENCES—PAST OR PAST-TO-PRESENT TIME

■ **ACTIVITY F** What if you had been born at a different time? How would your life have been different? What if you had been born in a different place? How would your life be different today? Test your knowledge in a game like Trivial Pursuit. Separate into four different groups. In your groups, make up questions about history, geography, languages, social customs, and so on. (Be sure that you know the answers!) The questions should use clauses with *if*.

Examples   **If you had lived in London in 1900, who would have been the ruler of your country? (Queen Victoria)**

If you had been in Buenos Aires in 1930, what kind of music might you have listened to? (tangos)

When you have prepared eight to ten questions, get together with another group. Take turns asking the other group your questions and answering theirs. Keep a count of correct answers. The group with the highest score wins.

■ **ACTIVITY G**   Poetry is a beautiful form of expression in any language, but it is often difficult to write. In poetry, every word plays an important role, so each must be chosen with care. Interestingly, it is sometimes easier to write poetry in a second or foreign language. A language learner can bring different perspectives and ideas to poetry and thus produce unusual combinations of words and images. Individually, in small groups, or as a whole class, use the following directions to help you write short poems. You may choose your own topic or select from the suggestions below. Follow the guidelines.

Before you begin writing, read the poem "A Smaller World." It is a class poem that was written by students from Mexico, Brazil, Japan, Colombia, Kuwait, Honduras, Switzerland, and Indonesia.

1. Write a poem about one of your classmates.
2. Write a poem about English (grammar, composition, etc.).
3. Write about an emotion or idea—love, friendship, homesickness, curiosity.
4. Write about a favorite place (a place here or in your country).

GUIDELINES

You need not follow these strictly.
Line 1. Write a sentence of three to five words about your topic.
Line 2. Take a noun from line 1 and describe it.
Line 3. Add movement to the idea in line 2.
Line 4. Pick a word in line 3 and compare it to something (*X is like* . . .).
Line 5. Take the idea in line 4 and describe it or add more action.
Line 6. Take the idea in line 5 and compare it to something (*X is* . . .).
Line 7. Make the idea in line 6 either very big or very small.
Line 8. Describe the idea in line 7.
Lines 9–10. End with a final statement or opinion.

A SMALLER WORLD

We came from so many places,

Gentle, crowded, warm, noisy, icy places,

Excited travelers, nervous and naive,

Like newborns entering a new world.

5 Babbling and blundering our way to English,

Like babies learning to talk.

Mountains of words, ideas, customs to climb,

A struggle for understanding.

Yet our world has become smaller

10 Because we have known each other.

—Class poem

▦ Appendices

Parts of Speech and Sentences

Every sentence in English is made up of basic components called "parts of speech": adjective, adverb, article, conjunction, noun, preposition, pronoun, and verb.

NOUN VERB ARTICLE ADVERB ADJECTIVE NOUN PRONOUN VERB PREPOSITION

Miriam is a very nice young woman. She comes from

NOUN CONJUNCTION PRONOUN VERB PREPOSITION ADJECTIVE NOUN

Venezuela, and she is studying   at   our school.

A sentence is a group of words that expresses a complete idea. Each sentence includes at least one subject and one verb.

Subjects

Noun or Pronoun	**Miriam** comes from Venezuela. **She** is from Caracas.	A noun names a person, place, thing, or idea. Pronouns replace nouns.

⟶

250

Phrase	**Many Venezuelan students** are studying in the United States. **To study in the United States** can be expensive. **Studying in the United States** can be expensive.	A phrase is a group of related words. Noun phrases or verb phrases may be used as subjects.
Clause	**How long they stay in the United States** depends on many things.	A clause is a group of related words that includes a subject and a verb.

Verbs, Objects, and Complements

Intransitive Verbs	Miriam **travels** often.	An intransitive verb is complete without an object.
Transitive Verbs and Objects	When she travels, she always **buys** souvenirs.	A transitive verb *must* have an object. It is incomplete without one.
Direct Object	She bought her daughter **a sweater.**	Direct objects answer the questions *Who(m)?* or *What?*
Indirect Object	She bought **her daughter** a sweater.	Indirect objects answer the questions *To/For who(m)? or What?*
Linking Verbs and Complements	Chato **is** an engineer. He **seems** happy with his work. It **appears** to be an interesting job.	Information that describes the subject follows linking verbs such as *appear, be, become,* and *feel.* The word, phrase, or clause that follows a linking verb is called a compound.

Pronouns and Possessive Adjectives

Subject	I	you	he	she	it	we	they
Object	me	you	him	her	it	us	them
Possessive Adjective	my	your	his	her	its	our	their
Possessive Pronoun	mine	yours	his	hers	its	ours	theirs
Reflexive Pronoun	myself	yourself	himself	herself	itself	ourselves	themselves

Principal Parts of Verbs

All tenses and other verb constructions are formed from the five principal parts of the verbs.

INFINITIVE	SIMPLE FORM	PAST FORM	PAST PARTICIPLE	PRESENT PARTICIPLE
to walk	walk	walked	walked	walking
to play	play	played	played	playing
to run	run	ran	run	running
to write	write	wrote	written	writing
to be	be	was/were	been	being
to do	do	did	done	doing
to have	have	had	had	having

The modal auxiliaries—*can, could, may, might, must, ought to, shall, should, will,* and *would*—are not included here because each has only *one* form, the simple form.

Verb Tense Formation

Simple Form   The simple form is used to form commands, the simple present tense, and the simple future tense. It is also used with modal auxiliaries.

COMMANDS	SIMPLE PRESENT	SIMPLE FUTURE
Stand!	I **walk.**	I **will walk.**
Be seated!	She **walks.**	She **will walk.**

Past Form   The past form is used for the simple past tense. Regular verbs are the simple form + -*ed*. Irregular verbs have changes in spelling and/or pronunciation.

REGULAR VERBS	IRREGULAR VERBS
I **walked**. She **walked**.	I **ran**. She **ran**.

Past Participle   The past participle is used to form the present, past, and future perfect tenses and all passive voice forms.

PRESENT PERFECT	PAST PERFECT	PASSIVE VOICE
I **have stopped**. She **has stopped**.	I **had stopped**. She **had stopped**.	It **was stopped**. They **will be stopped**.

Present Participle   The present participle is used with the verb *be* to form all continuous tenses. The -*ing* form can also act as a noun; in that case, it is called a *gerund*.

PRESENT CONTINUOUS	PAST CONTINUOUS	FUTURE CONTINUOUS
I **am resting**. She **is resting**. We **are resting**.	I **was resting**. She **was resting**. We **were resting**.	I **will be resting**. She **will be resting**. We **will be resting**.

PRESENT PERFECT CONTINUOUS	PAST PERFECT CONTINUOUS	FUTURE PERFECT CONTINUOUS
I **have been resting**. She **has been resting**.	I **had been resting**. She **had been resting**.	I **will have been resting**. She **will have been resting**.

Spelling Rules

SPELLING RULES FOR -*S*, -*ED*, -*ER*, -*EST*, AND -*ING* ENDINGS

This chart summarizes the basic spelling rules for endings with verbs, nouns, and adjectives.

RULE	WORD	-*s*	-*ed*	-*er*	-*est*	-*ing*
For most words, simply add -*s*, -*ed*, -*er*, -*est*, or -*ing* without making any other changes.	clean cool	cleans cools	cleaned cooled	cleaner cooler	cleanest coolest	cleaning cooling

Spelling changes occur with the following.

RULE	WORD	-*s*	-*ed*	-*er*	-*est*	-*ing*
For words ending in a consonant + *y*, change the *y* to *i* before adding -*s*, -*ed*, -*er*, or -*est*.	carry happy lonely study worry	carries studies worries	carried studied worried	carrier happier lonelier worrier	 happiest loneliest 	
Do *not* change or drop the y before adding -*ing*.						carrying studying worrying
For most words ending in *e*, drop the *e* before adding -*ed*, -*er*, -*est*, or -*ing*.	dance late nice save write		danced saved	dancer later nicer saver writer	 latest nicest	dancing saving writing
Exceptions:	agree canoe					agreeing canoeing

→

RULE	WORD	*-s*	*-ed*	*-er*	*-est*	*-ing*
For many words ending in one vowel and one consonant, double the final consonant before adding *-ed, -er, -est,* or *-ing.* These include one-syllable words and words with stress on the final syllable.	begin			beginner		beginning
	hot			hotter	hottest	
	mad			madder	maddest	
	plan		planned	planner		planning
	occur		occurred			occurring
	refer		referred			referring
	run			runner		running
	shop		shopped	shopper		shopping
	win			winner		winning
In words ending in one vowel and one consonant, do *not* double the final consonant if the last syllable is not stressed.	enter		entered			entering
	happen		happened			happening
	open		opened	opener		opening
	travel		traveled	traveler		traveling
	visit		visited			visiting
Exceptions: including words ending in *w, x,* or *y*	bus	buses	bused			busing
	fix		fixed	fixer		fixing
	play		played	player		playing
	sew		sewed	sewer		sewing
For most words ending in *f* or *lf,* change the *f* to *v* and add *-es.*	half	halves	halved			halving
	loaf	loaves				
	shelf	shelves	shelved	shelver		shelving
Exceptions:	belief	beliefs				
	chief	chiefs				
	proof	proofs				
	roof	roofs				
	safe	safes				
For words ending in *ch, sh, s, x, z,* and sometimes *o,* add *-es.*	church	churches				
	wash	washes				
	class	classes				
	fix	fixes				
	quiz	quizzes				
	tomato	tomatoes				
	zero	zeroes				
Exceptions:	dynamo	dynamos				
	ghetto	ghettos				
	piano	pianos				
	portfolio	portfolios				
	radio	radios				
	studio	studios				

⟶

IRREGULAR NOUN PLURALS

person	people	foot	feet	deer	deer	series	series
child	children	tooth	teeth	fish	fish	species	species
man	men			goose	geese		
woman	women			mouse	mice		
				ox	oxen		

NOUNS WITH FOREIGN ORIGINS

-is	*Changes to -es*	*-on or -um*	*Changes to -a*
analysis	analyses	bacterium	bacteria
basis	bases	criterion	criteria
crisis	crises	curriculum	curricula
hypothesis	hypotheses	datum	data
oasis	oases	medium	media
parenthesis	parentheses	memorandum	memoranda
synthesis	syntheses	phenomenon	phenomena
thesis	theses		

-us	*Changes to -i*	*Other*	
cactus	cacti **or** cactuses	formula	formulae **or** formulas
nucleus	nuclei	appendix	appendices **or** appen-dixes
radius	radii		
stimulus	stimuli	index	indices **or** indexes
syllabus	syllabi **or** syllabuses		

IRREGULAR VERBS

SIMPLE FORM	PAST	PAST PARTICIPLE
arise	arose	arisen
awake	awoke / awaked	awaked / awoken
be	was / were	been
bear	bore	borne / born
beat	beat	beat
become	became	become
begin	began	begun
bend	bent	bent
bet	bet	bet
bite	bit	bitten
bleed	bled	bled
blow	blew	blown

$\longrightarrow$

SIMPLE FORM	PAST	PAST PARTICIPLE
break	broke	broken
breed	bred	bred
bring	brought	brought
broadcast	broadcast	broadcast
build	built	built
burst	burst	burst
buy	bought	bought
cast	cast	cast
catch	caught	caught
choose	chose	chosen
cling	clung	clung
come	came	come
cost	cost	cost
creep	crept	crept
cut	cut	cut
deal	dealt	dealt
dig	dug	dug
do	did	done
draw	drew	drawn
drink	drank	drunk
drive	drove	driven
eat	ate	eaten
fall	fell	fallen
feed	fed	fed
feel	felt	felt
fight	fought	fought
find	found	found
flee	fled	fled
fly	flew	flown
forbid	forbade	forbidden
forget	forgot	forgotten
forsake	forsook	forsaken
freeze	froze	frozen
get	got	got / gotten
give	gave	given
go	went	gone
grind	ground	ground
grow	grew	grown
hang	hung / hanged	hung / hanged
have	had	had

$\longrightarrow$

SIMPLE FORM	PAST	PAST PARTICIPLE
hear	heard	heard
hide	hid	hidden
hit	hit	hit
hold	held	held
hurt	hurt	hurt
keep	kept	kept
know	knew	known
lay	laid	laid
lead	led	led
leave	left	left
lend	lent	lent
let	let	let
lie	lay	lain
light	lit / lighted	lit / lighted
lose	lost	lost
make	made	made
mean	meant	meant
meet	met	met
overcome	overcame	overcome
pay	paid	paid
prove	proved	proved / proven*
put	put	put
quit	quit	quit
read	read	read
ride	rode	ridden
ring	rang	rung
rise	rose	risen
run	ran	run
say	said	said
see	saw	seen
seek	sought	sought
sell	sold	sold
send	sent	sent
set	set	set
shake	shook	shaken
shoot	shot	shot

*These participles are most often used with the passive voice. $\longrightarrow$

SIMPLE FORM	PAST	PAST PARTICIPLE
show	showed	showed / shown*
shut	shut	shut
sing	sang	sung
sink	sank	sunk
sit	sat	sat
sleep	slept	slept
slide	slid	slid
slit	slit	slit
speak	spoke	spoken
spend	spent	spent
spin	spun	spun
split	split	split
spread	spread	spread
spring	sprang	sprung
stand	stood	stood
steal	stole	stolen
stick	stuck	stuck
sting	stung	stung
strike	struck	struck / stricken*
strive	strove	striven
swear	swore	sworn
sweep	swept	swept
swim	swam	swum
swing	swung	swung
take	took	taken
teach	taught	taught
tear	tore	torn
tell	told	told
think	thought	thought
throw	threw	thrown
thrust	thrust	thrust
understand	understood	understood
upset	upset	upset
wake	woke / waked	woken / waked
wear	wore	worn
weave	wove	woven
wind	wound	wound
withdraw	withdrew	withdrawn
write	wrote	written

*These participles are most often used with the passive voice.

Summary of Modal Auxiliaries and Related Structures

MODAL AUXILIARIES AND RELATED STRUCTURES

Modal Auxiliary	Function	PRESENT / FUTURE TIME FRAME
can	ability	**Can** you touch your toes without bending your knees?
	informal request	**Can** you teach me to swim?
could	request	**Could** I make an appointment with Dr. Saki?
	possibility	Perhaps Noriko **could** take you to the dentist.
may	request permission	**May** I leave now? Yes, you **may**.
	possibility	Sulaiman **may** be sick.
might	possibility	He **might** have the flu.
must	probability	He **must** be sick because he looks terrible.
	need	You **must** take this medicine immediately.
must not	strong need not to do something	You **must not** drive while you are taking this medicine.
ought to	advice	She **ought to** get more rest.
	expectation	The doctor **ought to** be here soon.
shall	request	**Shall** I get a bandage?
	intention	We **shall** probably go to the hospital later today.
should	advice	I **should** give up smoking.
	expectation	The swelling **should** go down in a few hours.
will	intention	I **will** get more exercise from now on!
would	request	**Would** you get me a bandage, please? **Would** you **mind** getting me a bandage?
	preference	**Would** you **like** a diet soda? I **would rather** have juice than soda.

$\longrightarrow$

Related Structure	Function	
be able to	ability	**Are** you **able to** swim three miles?
had better	advice	You **had better** not swim so soon after lunch.
have to (have got to)	need	I **have to (have got to)** lose weight.
don't/doesn't have to	lack of need	We **don't have to** get X rays. He **doesn't have to** take any medicine.

PAST TIME FRAME

Modal Auxiliary	Function	
could	ability	I **could** not swim until last year.
could have	possibility	I **could have** taken lessons sooner.
may have	possibility	They **may** already **have** gone to the hospital.
might have	possibility	Juan **might have** injured his back when he fell.
must have	probability	He **must have** been in a lot of pain.
ought to have	advice not taken expectation	He **ought to have** been more careful. The doctor **ought to have** called us by now.
should have	advice not taken expectation	**Should** we **have** waited for help? Someone **should have** arrived by now.
would	habits	When I was younger, I **would** always faint at the sight of blood.
would have	preference	I **would have** liked to visit her. She **would** rather not **have** visited the hospital.
	intention not completed	Under other circumstances, **would** you **have** had that operation?

Related Structure	Function	
be able to	ability	Nadia **was able to** run two miles.
didn't have to	lack of need	We **didn't have to** practice on Monday because of the rain.
had to	need	We **had to** practice twice as long yesterday because we missed practice on Monday.
used to	habits	We **used to** eat a lot of sugar, but we don't anymore.

The with Proper Nouns

THE WITH PROPER NOUNS

With the		Without the	
The is used when the class of noun (continent, country, etc.) comes before the name: *the* + class + *of* + name.	the continent of Asia the United States of America the U.S.A.	*The* is not used with names of planets, continents, countries, states, provinces, cities, and streets.	Mars Africa Antarctica Russia Ohio Quebec Austin State Street
The is used with most names of regions. *Exceptions:*	the West the Midwest the equator New England southern (northern, eastern, etc.) Ontario	*Exceptions:*	(the) earth the world the Netherlands the Sudan the Hague the Champs-Élysées
The is used with plural islands, lakes, and mountains. *The* is used with oceans, seas, rivers, canals, deserts, jungles, forests, and bridges.*	the Hawaiian Islands the Great Lakes the Alps the Pacific Ocean the Persian Gulf the Mississippi River the Suez Canal the Sahara Desert the Black Forest the Golden Gate Bridge	*The* is not used with singular islands, lakes, and mountains. *Exceptions:*	Oahu Fiji Lake Superior Mt. Whitney Pikes Peak the Isle of Wight the Great Salt Lake the Matterhorn (and other mountains with German names that are used in English)

* The class name is often omitted with well-known oceans, deserts, and rivers: *the Atlantic, the Nile.*

With the		Without the	
The is generally used when the word *college, university,* or *school* comes before the name: *the* + . . . + *of* + name.	the University of California the Rhode Island School of Design	*The* is not used when the name of a college or university comes before the word *college* or *university*. *Exception:*	Boston University Amherst College the Sorbonne
The is used with adjectives of nationality and other adjectives that function as nouns.	the Germans the Japanese the rich the poor the hungry the strong	*The* is not used with names of languages. *Note: The* is used with the word *language: the German language.*	German Japanese
The is used in dates when the number comes before the month.	the twenty-eighth of March	*The* is not used in dates when the month begins the phrase.	March 28
The is used with decades, centuries, and eras.	the 1990s the 1800s the Dark Ages	*The* is not used with specific years.	1951 1890
The is used with names of museums and libraries.	the Museum of Modern Art the Chicago Public Library		

Summary of Gerunds and Infinitives

VERBS OFTEN FOLLOWED BY GERUNDS

admit	She **admitted** stealing the money.
anticipate	We **anticipate** arriving late.
appreciate	I really **appreciated** getting your card.
avoid	She **avoids** stepping on cracks — a superstition.
be worth	I am sure it **is worth** waiting.
can(not) help	He **can't help** getting upset about that.
consider	Have you **considered** moving?
delay	They **delayed** starting the game because of the rain.
deny	He **denied** speeding.
dislike	He really **dislikes** getting up early.
dread	She **dreads** going to the dentist.
enjoy	We always **enjoy** traveling.
escape	We narrowly **escaped** hitting the other car.
finish	Have you **finished** writing that paper?
forgive	I can **forgive** his cheating, but I can't **forgive** his lying.
imagine	Can you **imagine** living in Bogotá?
involve	This job **involves** meeting a lot of people.
keep (on)	**Keep on** working until I tell you to stop.
mention	Did she **mention** quitting her job?
miss	I **miss** hearing your voice.
postpone	Will they **postpone** calling a meeting?
practice	A good tennis player has to **practice** serving.
recommend	I **recommend** taking some aspirin.
regret	I **regret** saying that.
risk	She **risked** losing all her money in that deal.
spend (time)	Do you **spend** much **time** doing your homework?
suggest	They **suggested** having a picnic.
tolerate	I can't **tolerate** listening to rock music.
understand	Do you **understand** his not calling?

VERBS OFTEN FOLLOWED BY INFINITIVES

SUBJECT + VERB + INFINITIVE

afford	We can't **afford** to go.
agree	They **agreed** to help.
appear	She **appeared** to be calm, but she was quite nervous.
be	We **were** to do the homework in Chapter 3.
be able	**Were** you **able** to finish the work?
be supposed	You **were supposed** to do it yesterday.
care	I don't **care** to go.
decide	He **decided** to stay.
deserve	She **deserves** to get a high grade.
fail	They **failed** to make the announcement.
forget	I **forgot** to buy eggs.
happen	Did he **happen** to stop by?
have	I **have** to leave.
hesitate	Don't **hesitate** to call!
hope	We **hope** to visit Rome next spring.
intend	I **intend** to stop there for several days.
know how	Do you **know how** to play squash?
learn	She **is learning** to play tennis.
manage	Somehow he **managed** to finish the race.
offer	They **offered** to help us.
plan	We **planned** to leave earlier.
prepare	They **prepared** to get on board the plane.
pretend	He **pretended** not to notice us.
refuse	I **refuse** to get up at 5:00 A.M.!
seem	He **seems** to be upset.
tend	She **tends** to forget things.
threaten	The employee **threatened** to quit.
volunteer	Several people **volunteered** to help us.
wait	She **waited** for the letter carrier to come.
wish	We **wished** to go, but we couldn't.

	SUBJECT + VERB + (OPTIONAL NOUN OR PRONOUN) + INFINITIVE
ask	We **asked** to come. We **asked** them to come.
beg	He **begged** to go. He **begged** us to go.
dare	I **dared** to go. I **dared** him to go.
expect	I **expect** to finish soon. I **expect** them to finish soon.
need	I **need** to go. I **need** you to go.
promise	She **promised** to help. She **promised** her mother to help.
want	They **want** to leave. They **want** us to leave.
would like	He **would like** to stay. He **would like** you to stay.
use	They **used** to live there. (habitual past) They **used** a hammer to fix the table. (method)

	SUBJECT + VERB + NOUN OR PRONOUN + INFINITIVE
advise*	The doctor **advised** me to rest.
allow*	He won't **allow** you to swim.
cause*	The accident **caused** me to faint.
convince	She **convinced** us to try again.
encourage*	I **encourage** you to study languages.
force	The hijacker **forced** them to land the plane.
get	He **got** them to pay ransom.
hire	We **hired** you to do the job.
invite	They **invited** us to come.
order	I **am ordering** you to stop!
permit*	**Will** they **permit** us to camp here?
persuade	Perhaps we can **persuade** them to let us go.
remind	Did you **remind** her to buy milk?
require	The school **required** us to wear uniforms.

---

* These verbs are followed by gerunds if no noun or pronoun object is used after the main verb.

SUBJECT + VERB + NOUN OR PRONOUN + INFINITIVE

teach*	He **taught** me to play tennis.
tell	I **told** him not to come.
urge	We **urge** you to change your mind.
warn	I **am warning** you to stop!

VERB + GERUND OR INFINITIVE (*SAME MEANING*)

begin	She **began** to work (working) on the project.
can't bear	I **can't bear** to see (seeing) her work so much.
can't stand	She **can't stand** to stay (staying) alone at night.
continue	They'll **continue** to practice (practicing) several days more.
hate	He **hates** to play (playing) golf.
like	I **like** to play (playing) tennis.
love	Mary **loves** to read (reading) novels.
neglect	We **neglected** to tell (telling) her about that.
prefer	I **prefer** to go (going) alone.
start	We **started** to worry (worrying) about the situation.

VERB + GERUND OR INFINITIVE (*DIFFERENT MEANINGS*)

mean	I **meant** to finish the project sooner. This **means** delaying the project.
quit (stop)	He **quit (stopped)** to take a long break. We **quit (stopped)** taking breaks in order to leave work earlier.
remember	**Did** you **remember** to tell her? I **remember** telling her about it, but she forgot.
try	We **tried** to call you, but the phone was out of order. I **tried** calling, and then I decided to write you a note.

---

* These verbs are followed by gerunds if no noun or pronoun object is used after the main verb.

Index

Ability, 66–67
 expressing, 46–50, 66
Abstract nouns, 92
Active voice, 71
Adjective clauses, 191–215
 object replacement with *who(m)* and *which*,
  207–212
 possessives replacement with *whose*,
  204–206
 restrictive and nonrestrictive, 200–201
 subject replacement with, 212
 subject replacement with *who* or *which*,
  202–204
 with *that*, 194–195
 with *when* or *where*, 195–196
Adjectives
 comparisons with, 163–166
 indefinite, 98–103
 and infinitives, 123
 participles used as, 145–146
 possessive, 252
Adverb clauses, 151–190
 of time, 156–159, 180–181
Adverbials, replacement of, 195–196
Adverbs
 comparisons with, 163–166
 of frequency, 7–9
 and infinitives, 122
 in past tense, 31
 and reported speech, 223–224
Advice, 59–61, 67
A lot (of), 101
Articles
 definite, 104–109
 indefinite, 95
 nouns without, 113
 the, 107–109
Auxiliaries, 260–261

Be going to, 22–23
By (and agent), 74–77

Causative verbs and related structures,
  141–150

Cause, clauses and, 169–173, 189–190
Clauses. *See also* Adjective clauses
 adjective, 191–215
 adverb, 151–190
 noun, 216–249, 226–230
 restrictive and nonrestrictive, 199–206
 showing cause, contrast, purpose, and result
  or effect, 169–179, 189–190
 showing comparison, 166–169
 showing contrast, 173–174
 of time, 179–187, 189–190
Comparisons, 162–169
 with adjectives and adverbs, 163–166
 clauses and phrases showing, 166–169
Complements, 251
Complex sentences, 155
Compound sentences, 154
Concession, 173–174
Conditional sentences
 hope, wish, and, 231–236
 imaginative past time, 240–241
 imaginative with *if*, 242
 noun clauses and, 216–249
 perfect modal auxiliaries and, 237–245
Continuous tenses
 future, 25
 passive voice and, 80–83
 past, 42
 present, 9–13
Contrast, clauses, phrases, and, 169–173,
  189–190
Could, 238
Count nouns, 91, 93–94, 96–98, 99, 100–101,
  113–114
 and definite article, 104–106
 indefinite adjectives and pronouns and, 99

Definite article, with count and noncount
  nouns, 104–109
Direct object, 251

Effect, clauses, and phrases, 169–173, 189–190
Expectation, expressing, 46, 48–49, 66

Feelings, verbs for, 11
Few, 102
    modifiers with, 101–103
Frequency, 7–9
Future. *See also Wish*
Future continuous tense, 25–26, 42
Future tense, simple, 23, 43
Future time, clauses of, 187–188

Generalizations, 113
Gerunds, 264–267
    with adjective-preposition combinations,
        148
    and expressions with *to*, 119
    forms of, 117–120
    and infinitives, 149
    and prepositions, 118
    verbs followed by. *See* Verbs
Get, 142

Had to, expressing past needs with, 67
Have, 142
Have to, expressing present needs with, 67
Help, 141
Hope
    conditional sentences and, 231–236
    versus *wish*, 246

Identified nouns, 105–106
If
    in conditional sentences, 160
    imaginative conditional sentences with, 242
    noun clauses with, 227
Indefinite adjectives, 98–103
    and count and noncount nouns, 99
Indefinite article, 95
Indefinite pronouns, 98–103
    and count and noncount nouns, 99
Indirect object, 251
Infinitives, 121–125, 264–267
    active vs. passive, 122
    adverbs, adjectives, and nouns and, 122–125
    and gerunds, 149
    verbs followed by. *See* Verbs
Intransitive verbs, 251
Irregular adjectives and adverbs, 164
Irregular verbs, spelling of, 256–259

Let, 141
Linking verbs, 251

Little, a, 100–101
    modifiers with, 101–102

Make, 141
May, 238
Measurement, units of, 109–113
Modal auxiliaries, 44–67, 260–261
    of ability and expectation, 46–50, 66
    conditional sentences and, 237–245
    of need and advice, 55–61, 67
    passive voice and, 83–86
    of possibility and probability, 61–65
    of preference, 53–55, 66–67
    quotation, reported speech, and, 220
    in reported speech, 224–226
    of request, permission, and preference,
        50–55, 66–67
Modifiers, 101–103

Need, 55–58, 67, 142
Noncount nouns, 100–101, 113–114, 92–94,
    96–98
    and definite article, 106–109
    indefinite adjectives and pronouns and, 99
Nonrestrictive adjective clauses, 200–201
(*Not*) *many*, 100–101
(*Not*) *much*, 100–101
Noun clauses
    clause to phrase reduction, 226–230
    and conditional sentences, 216–249
    with *if* and *whether*, 227
    with question words, 228
    and reported speech, 218–226, 245
Noun object, and infinitives, 132–135. *See
    also* Gerunds
Nouns, 89–98
    abstract, 92
    without articles, 113
    by and, 75
    concrete mass, 92
    count, 113–114, 91, 93–94, 96–98, 99
    identified or specified, 105–106
    and infinitives, 123
    noncount, 113–114, 92–94, 96–98
    proper, 107–109
    the with, 262–263

Objects, 251
    replacement of, 213

Objects of prepositions, replacement of, 209–212
Objects of verbs
  replacement of, 196–198, 207–212
Only, 102
Opposition, 173–174
Ought to, 238

Participles, as adjectives, 145. *See also* Gerunds
Parts of speech, and sentences, 250–253
  continuous tenses, 80–83
  formation of, 71
  modal auxiliaries, 83–86
  perfect tenses, 77–80
  simple tenses, 70–77, 72–73
Past. *See also Wish*
Past perfect tense, 35, 38–41, 78
Past tense, 253
  continuous, 42
  perfect, 35–41
  simple, 38, 42, 87
Past time
  and imaginative conditional sentences, 240–241
  showing, 180–181
Perception, verbs of, 11, 144, 150
Perfect continuous tense, 27–28, 43
Perfect modal auxiliaries, 238–240
Perfect tenses, 77–80
Permission, 50–53, 66
Phrases
  showing cause, purpose, and effect or result, 170
  showing comparison, 166–169
  showing contrast, 173–174
Place, adjective clauses and, 195–196
Possession, verbs for, 12
Possessive adjectives, 252
Possessives, replacement of, 204–206
Possibility, 61–65
Preference, 53–55, 66–67
Prepositions
  gerunds and, 118, 148
  replacement of objects of, 209–212
Present. *See also Wish*
Present continuous tense, 3, 9–13, 41
Present participles, gerunds and, 117
Present perfect continuous tense, 27–28
Present perfect tense, 27, 28–34, 43, 78

Present tense, adverbs with, 31
Present time, clauses of, 187–188
Probability, 61–65
Pronoun object, and infinitives, 132–135. *See also* Gerunds
Pronouns, 89, 98–103, 252
  by and, 75
  indefinite, 98–103
  and reported speech, 223–224
Proper nouns
  the with, 107–109, 262–263
Purpose, clauses, phrases, and, 169–173, 189–190

Questions, embedded, 226, 228, 246
Question words, noun clauses with, 228
Quite, 101
Quotations, 219–223

Relative pronoun, 196–197
Reported speech, 218–226, 245
  pronoun and speech changes in, 223–224
  verbs, modal auxiliaries, and, 224–226
Request, 50–53, 66
Restrictive adjective clauses, 200–201
Result, clauses, phrases, and, 169–173, 189–190

Say versus *tell*, 223
Sentences
  conditional, 216–249, 231–245
  parts of speech and, 250–253
  types of, 154–156
  for unspecified or present time, 159–160
Should, 238
Simple future tense, 23, 43
Simple past tense, 38, 42, 87
Simple present tense, 3, 4–6, 41
Simple sentences, 154
Simple tenses
  future tense, 23, 43
  passive voice and, 70–77
  past tense, 38, 42, 87
  present tense, 3, 4–6, 41
Specified nouns, 105–106
Speech, reported, 218–226
Spelling rules, 254–255
  for *-ed* endings, 14
  for *-ing* endings, 18
  for *-s* endings, 5

Spelling rules (*Cont.*)
  for irregular noun plurals, 256
  for nouns with foreign origins, 256
Subjects, 250–251
  replacement of, 194, 202–204, 212
Subjunctive mood, 231

Tell versus *say*, 223
Tenses, 1–43. *See also* Past time
  continuous, 80–83
  contrast of, 34, 87
  formation of verb, 252–253
  future, 22–26
  passive voice, 70–77
  past continuous, 13, 18–22, 42
  past perfect, 35–41
  perfect, 77–80
  present continuous, 3, 9–13, 42
  sequence of in reported speech, 219–223
  simple past, 13, 14–17, 38, 42, 87
  simple present, 3, 4–6, 41
That
  adjective clauses with, 194–195, 196–198
The, with proper nouns, 107–109
Thoughts, verbs for, 11
Time
  adjective clauses and, 195–196
  adverb clauses of, 156–159
  clauses of, 179–187, 189–190
  conditional sentences and, 235–236
  factual conditional sentences for, 159–160
  hope, wish, conditional sentences and,
    231–236
  modal auxiliaries, conditional sentences,
    and, 237–245
  present or future, 187–188
Time expressions, 4, 7, 28, 30, 38
Transitions, showing cause, purpose, and
  effect or result, 171
Transitive verbs, 71, 251

Units of measurement, 109–113
Unless, in conditional sentences, 161
Used to, 35–36

Verb forms, 115–150
  irregular past, 14
Verbs
  causative, 141–150
  followed by gerunds or infinitives, 126–140
  irregular, 256–259
  meaning changes, infinitives, and, 138–140
  and objects, 251
  participle forms of, 145
  of perception, 144, 150
  principal parts of, 252
  in reported speech, 224–226
  transitive, 71
Verb tense formation, 252–253
Verb tenses, 1–43
  future, 22–26
  past perfect, 35–41
  present continuous, 3–13
  present perfect, 27, 28–34
  present perfect continuous, 27–28
  simple past, 13, 14–17
  simple present, 3–13
  third person singular, 6
Very, 102
Vocabulary, 2, 69–70, 116, 152, 192–193,
    217–218
Voice. *See also* Tenses
  active, 71
  passive, 68–88

Was/were going to, 35, 36–38
Were going to, 35, 36–38
When, adjective clauses with, 195–196
When versus *while*, 13, 20–22
Where, adjective clauses with, 195–196
Whether, noun clauses with, 227
Which, 202–203, 207–212
Who, 202–203
Whom, 207–212
Whose, 204–206
Wish
  conditional sentences and, 231–236
  hope and, 246
Would, 35–36, 238